A HYMN TO SATAN

A HYMN TO SATAN
& OTHER TRANSLATED POEMS
by
GIOSUÈ CARDUCCI

WITH INTRODUCTORY ESSAYS BY
R. MERCILESS &
G. L. BICKERSTETH

TRANSLATIONS BY
G.L. BICKERSTETH & EMILY A. TRIBE

UNDERWORLD AMUSEMENTS

Cover art: *Les fleurs du mal* by Armand Seguin, 1892

This edition designed and edited by Kevin I. Slaughter
for Underworld Amusements.

"Giosuè Carducci: 19th Century Poet, Statesman and Satanist", © by
R. Merciless.

Additional thanks to the Church of Satan for permission to print "Gio-
suè Carducci" by R. Merciless. The essay first appeared on their website
ChurchOfSatan.com.

UNDERWORLD AMUSEMENTS
WWW.UNDERWORLDAMUSEMENTS.COM
978-1-943687-01-5

Notes on the Translation

I have selected just under seventy of Carducci's poems as I thought best represented his genius in all its aspects. Personal preference for this rather than for that poem has, of course, to a large extent influenced my choice. As to what were his masterpieces, I have also been guided by the opinion, as expressed in anthologies, of the poet's own countrymen. But several poems—notably the selections from *Giambi ed Epodi*—are included in this book for no other reason than that they serve to illustrate the various stages through which Carducci passed in the long course of his development both as man and poet.

I have provided all the poems in this book with verse translations, about which a word of explanation is necessary.

Any one who ventures to translate Italian poetry must soon become acutely conscious of the truth contained in Dante's well-known warning: *"Nulla cosa per legame musaico armonizzata si pub della sua loquela in altra trasmutare senza rompere tutta sua dolcezza e armonia"* (*Convito,* i. 7). It is hardly necessary for me to say that I do not put forward the translations in this book as in any sense an equivalent of their originals. The ideal translator of poetry must not only be a poet himself, but must probably also be capable of writing poetry in the language which he is translating. Translation, however, may be practised as one of the useful arts by those who lay no claim to be themselves poets. It constitutes indeed a very valuable addition to the equipment of the critic, besides being a fascinating occupation in itself. My versions of these poems were not made for those who can read the Italian at sight. Written in the first place to satisfy myself that I understood the poet's meaning, I hope that they will serve not as a substitute for, but as an interpretation of, the original to those unacquainted or only slightly acquainted with the Italian language. So far as my own knowledge and skill went, I have tried to render faithfully at once the substance, the form, and the spirit of the Italian. The Notes to the poems have been made as brief as possible, and are only meant to explain the more obscure of the literary and historical allusions with which Carducci's poetry abounds.

No translator, I imagine, is ever satisfied with his work, and I can only express regret that so many blemishes still mar what I have done my best to make a worthy interpretation of Carducci to English readers.

G. L. Bickersteth.

Marlborough, England.
June 1913.

Notes on Editing

The bulk of this volume is derived from the earlier *Carducci: A Selection of His Poems, With Verse Translations* by G.L. Bickersteth (1913). That edition contained the original Italian as well as the translated poems, and I have decided to not include the originals for any but the titular poem.

For "Hymn to Satan", along with the Italian, I have also included a second English translation by Emily A. Tribe, from her 1921 collection *A Selection From the Poems of Giosuè Carducci*.

This volume is prepared for a largely monolingual American audience, and, even for myself, the inclusion of the original Italian for every poem would merely consume space without benefit. The benefit of removing these from my own volume is to give space to the English translations. Now there is room to allow the poems to begin and end on their own pages, instead of flowing one right after the other, as in the original.

In the front matter, I have also made some editorial changes. I have edited Bickersteth's "Preface" to deal only with his notes pertaining to his translation work, omitting his personal "thank you" list and digressions. Where he produced three introductory essays, I have only included one. The first of his was a biographical sketch of Carducci. It has been replaced with a modern introduction by R. Merciless, who also ties the author and his work to Satanism, a philosophy the editor is associated with. The third was a rather overly long and technical discussion of the "Meteres of the *Barbarian Odes*". Being dry and specific only to part of the book, I will leave the interested reader to study on their own.

I have retained Bickersteth's British spelling, but updated the punctuation where needed. Further, where quotes and excerpts are untranslated, I have left them that way.

Kevin I. Slaughter.
Baltimore, MD.
December, 2017.

TABLE OF CONTENTS

RIME E RITMI

CANZONE DI LEGNANO

x

Giosuè Carducci:
19th Century Poet, Statesman and Satanist

In 1906 the Nobel Prize for literature was awarded to Giosuè Carducci of Italy for extraordinary lifelong accomplishment in the field of poetry. He was a Satanist.

By the time he won the Nobel, Carducci had firmly established himself as one of the world's most well-known and influential literary figures with a large body of distinguished work and a long career of artistic achievement, political activism and religious agitation. He had published several volumes of poetry attracting worldwide critical acclaim. In addition, his prose writings including literary criticism, biographies, speeches and essays filled some 20 volumes.[1] He had also been elected a Senator of Italy and voted a very substantial life-long pension. The Nobel prize was merely the capstone of a long, brilliant and highly successful life.[2]

Carducci's credentials as a Satanist include not only his worldly successes and overt opposition to Christianity but his writing of the highly controversial poem, *Inno a Satana* or "Hymn to Satan." In writing, publicly reciting and twice publishing this astounding poem, he stepped firmly beyond his paganism and even his anti-clericalism into the realm of modern Satanism by embracing the mythic character of Satan as an exemplary role model and heroic archetypal symbol. Indeed, it is this taking of Satan as an exemplar symbol that is the defining characteristic of the Modern Satanist.[3]

Of course, living as he did in 19th century Italy, Carducci probably would not have referred to himself as a "Satanist." The linking of that term to the Satanic character would have to wait almost exactly 100 more years when Anton Szandor LaVey, founder of The Church of Satan, defined it for the modern world in The Satanic Bible in 1969.[4] Nonetheless, Carducci's explicit and life-long adoption of Satan as archetypically symbolic of his personal philosophy which he called "radical rationalism," unequivocally places the Nobel laureate firmly within the Satanic tradition, even if less daring biographers have

---

1   Carducci, Giosuè, *Selections from Carducci; Prose and Poetry with introduction, notes and vocabulary* by A. Marinoni, (William R. Jenkins Co.; New York) 1913. pp vii - ix

2   Scalia, Samuel Eugene, *Carducci*, (S.F. Vanni, Inc., New York) 1937.

3   LaVey, Anton Szandor, *The Satanic Bible*, (Avon, New York) 1969. p 25

4   Barton, Blanche, *The Church of Satan*, (Hells Kitchen, New York) 1990. p 60

preferred the term "pagan" to describe him.

Carducci felt great affinity for the classical world and wrote several internationally acclaimed homages to ancient Roman gods and the long lost, Christian-obliterated happy pagan lifestyle of old. But unlike Baudelair, Leopardi, Levi, Rimbaud, Huysmans and other 19th century literary figures who penned somewhat Satanic works, Carducci did not die on his knees whimpering and begging forgiveness from a previously scorned Christian god.[1] Instead, he died an unabashed enemy of the Pope and ended his days as defiantly anti-clerical as he ever was.

Carducci was born near Verana, Italy in 1835. From an early age, guided by his politically active physician father, he learned Latin and studied the Iliad and classical works of Homer. He also energetically read the works of the famous Italian poet, Giacomo Leopardi (1798 - 1837) and was perhaps somewhat inspired towards *Inno a Satana* by reading the despondent Leopardi's unfinished *Ad Ahrimane* ("To Ahriman,") an at times depressing prayer addressed to the Prince of Darkness and acknowledging His rule of the Earth.[2]

By 1860, at age 25, he had been appointed to the chair in Italian Literature at Bologna University where he would spend a long, brilliant career of over 40 years. He was also actively involved in the political upheavals reshaping Italy at the time.

It was a time of revolution in Italy as Republicans, inspired and assisted by revolutionary France, struggled to throw off the old tyrannical Hapsburg order and unite and democratize Italy's many separate feudal states and kingdoms. By the mid-1860s, after years of civil war and political struggle most of the Italian peninsula had been united under a constitutional republican monarchy. However, one of the last vestiges of tyrannical domination on the Italian peninsula was the continued direct political control of Rome and surrounding regions by the Pope. With the military backing of Hapsburg Austria, the Pope held direct secular political power over the Italian provinces known as the Papal States. Naturally, the anti-clerical freethinkers among the Republicans found tyrannical rule by the papacy to be as

1   Regarding the later day Christianity of Baudelaire see Russell, Jeffrey Burton, *Mephistopheles: The Devil in the Modern World*, (Cornell University Press; Ithaca, New York) 1986. p 208. Regarding Rimbaud, see Russell p 209. Regarding Levi, see Waite's preface of Levi, Eliphas, *The History of Magic* translated by A.E. Waite, (Samuel Weiser, Inc., York Beach, ME) 1913 p. 7.

2   Zacharias, Gerhard, *The Satanic Cult*, transl. by Christine Trollope, (George Allen & Unwin, London) 1964. p.125

odious as, or even worse than, that by unelected, hereditary nobles. Both impeded human progress by locking power in the hands of those who were long on hereditary or ecclesiastical connections and short on any actual demonstrated merit or ability.

Throughout Italy, 19th century Masonic lodges were centers of organizing revolutionary activities ranging from anti-royalist propaganda to underground guerrilla attacks. Carducci was, of course, a member as were nearly all the other significant leaders of the Italian revolutionary movement. Other prominent masons of the time included influential political philosopher Giuseppe Mazinni, head of the successful Young Italy movement, and Giuseppe Garibaldi, the internationally famous Italian revolutionary war hero.

In contrast to the overtly theistic and even Christian flavor to be found among German and Anglo-American Freemasons at the time, French and Italian masonry both adopted a much more pan-religious, nearly overtly atheist tone. Like Masons everywhere, they too used the term "Grand Architect of the Universe" to refer to the "creator." For many of the more sharp-witted Italian and French Masons, however, it had a very different meaning. Applauding its own expansive view of the Mason's "Grand Architect", the official newsletter of the Italian lodge noted,

> "The formula of the Grand Architect, which is reproached to Masonry as ambiguous and absurd, is the most large-minded and righteous affirmation of the immense principle of existence and may represent as well the (revolutionary) God of Mazzini as the Satan of Giosuè Carducci (in his celebrated Hymn to Satan); God, as the fountain of love, not of hatred; Satan, as the genius of the good, not of the bad."[1]

This Masonic newsletter reference to Carducci in the same breath as Mazzini, one of the republic's most effective and inspiring revolutionary thinkers and leaders, clearly demonstrates Carducci's great prominence and influence at the time. Moreover, the sort of religious outlook quoted above made all of Italian masonry an explicit enemy of the Vatican. On March 18, 1902, Pope Leo XIII issued "Annum ingressi," a pronouncement against Italian Freemasonry. Of the above quotation, The Catholic Encyclopedia of 1910 disapprovingly sniffed, "In both interpretations it is in reality the principle of Revolution that is adored by Italian Masonry."

---

1   *Rivista*, 1909, p 44

The deep anti-church sentiment of French masons—most likely shared in full by their Italian brothers—is amply reflected in the following quote from a 20 September, 1902 speech by Senator Delpech, president of the Grand Orient de France:

> "The triumph of the Galilean has lasted twenty centuries. But now he dies in his turn. The mysterious voice, announcing (to Julian the Apostate) the death of Pan, today announces the death of the impostor God who promised an era of justice and peace to those who believe in him. The illusion has lasted a long time. The mendacious God is now disappearing in his turn; he passes away to join in the dust of ages the divinities of India, Egypt, Greece, and Rome, who saw so many creatures prostrate before their altars. Bro. Masons, we rejoice to state that we are not without our share in this overthrow of the false prophets. The Romish Church, founded on the Galilean myth, began to decay rapidly from the very day on which the Masonic Association was established."[1]

Carducci, the firebrand masonic freethinker and revolutionary, wrote Inno a Satana in September 1863, at the age of 28 and three years into his teaching chair at the University of Bologna. It was composed as a brindisi or toast which he recited at a dinner party among friends.[2] Appropriately for reciting with a raised glass of chianti, the poet titled it "A Satana" or "To Satan." It was then published in 1865 under the title *Inno a Satana* or "Hymn to Satan" but should probably have more accurately carried the title of "A Toast to Satan." The tone, rhyme, meter and content all bear this out clearly and well-reflect the origination of the work. It is not difficult to imagine a table full of Carducci's freethinking revolutionary pals hoisting their glasses at the conclusion of the recitation, shouting "Here, here," and quaffing a glass of Italy's finest produce. In vino veritas, indeed!

Modern literary scholars have recognized Inno a Satana as an in-your-face manifesto of Carducci's most deeply felt convictions and cherished beliefs, which he occasionally modified but never abandoned over the course of his long life. For Carducci, like for LaVey, Satan symbolically represents all of those wonderful things which the hierarchy of orthodox Christianity opposes and attempts to suppress:

---

1   *Compte-redu Grand Orient de France*, 1902. p 381
2   Carducci, Giosuè, *Selected Verse/ Giosuè Carducci: edited with a translation, introduction and commentary by David H. Higgins*, (Aris & Phillips; Warminster, England) 1994. pp34-47, 227-229

beauty in nature and art, sensual pleasures, confidence in man's ability to transform the physical world, freedom of thought and expression, unprejudiced intellectual inquiry, economic and social progress.

It is unfortunate that an English-reading person of the 21st century is not able fully to grasp the emotional power the poem invoked in 19th century Italy with its clever rhyming language and allusions to well-known recent and historical events and figures. Still, it can serve as an inspiration to others. Indeed, a glimmer of the impact can be discerned by seeing it (and even trying to read it aloud) in its original Italian. All readers should try this.

Readers will note that Carducci's poem includes 50 stanzas of 4 lines each where the second and fourth are rhymed. This meter seems to resonate something like a a train's locomotive steaming along under full power and this is a metaphor which the poet brings around the bend into full view at the close of the poem.

It was published a second time in 1869 in Bologna's radical newspaper, Il Popolo, as a provocation timed to coincide with the 20th Vatican Ecumenical Council, a time when revolutionary fervor directed against the papacy was running high as republicans were pressing both politically and militarily for an end of the Vatican's domination over the so-called papal states under the military support of the hated Austrian Hapsburgs.

The second publication was meant to be a provocation and provocative it was. Reaction to the reappearance of the controversial poem was quite strong. Even some of Carducci's fellow republicans publicly distanced themselves from embracing Satan along with the poet even if they were opposed to the Pope. Moderate newspapers excoriated Carducci for potentially harming the cause with such blasphemous and inflammatory writings.

But, in fact, the republican cause was triumphant. In 1870, Hapsburg Austrian military support for the Pope collapsed and republican troops marched into Rome, ending by force the papacy's secular political control of the region. It is quite likely that, as they took the city, at least some of those troops had Inno a Satana fresh in their minds.

But, as moderate republicans had feared, the Vatican seized upon the poem as a propaganda item. As Carducci introduced Satan as a worthy and honorable symbol of the republican opposition to the tyrannical earthly power of the papacy, the Vatican's propaganda to its faithful sheep painted the revolutionaries as accursed minions of the literal Devil. The 1910 Catholic Encyclopedia proclaimed Masonic

Lodges to be:

"...the advanced outposts and standard-bearers of the whole immense anti-Catholic and anti-papal army in the world-wide spiritual warfare of our age. In this sense also the pope, like the Masonic poet Carducci in his Hymn to Satan, considers Satan as the supreme spiritual chief of this hostile army."[1]

Clearly the Catholic Church stewed with such great frustration and hatred for the masons' anti-clerical activity, that it's disdain for Carducci in particular was never far from mind as indicated in the above passage. Had he lived to read it, Carducci would have no doubt been pleased to see his name thus immortalized in the Catholic Encyclopedia as a leading enemy of the church.

While Inno a Satana was extremely effective as a political device it was not considered by scholars and critics—or even by Carducci—to be great art. In the middle part of a major Oxford University lecture on Carducci's work in 1926, scholar John Baily, for example, offered the following analysis of *Inno a Satana*:

"It is at the bottom [Carducci's] faith in a sound mind and healthy body, [his] scorn of weaklings and palterers, which is the inspiration of the famous, or notorious Hymn to Satan. I cannot, of course, discuss it here from the point of view of religion. It gave and no doubt was meant to give, great offence to Catholics and indeed to all Christians—and still does. We must admit that he was always definitely a pagan: and often, especially in the first half of his life, not merely a pagan but an anti-Christian. This attitude is seen at its height in the Hymn to Satan though the title is, as we shall see, a misnomer. But to judge it or him fairly we must remember the time and place in which he wrote: an Italy which had long been ruled by priests who allied themselves with foreigners and tyrants, in which the Pope who had deserted the national cause still held Rome; in which one Pope had declared the steam engine to be an invention of the Devil and another was now replying to the spirit of the nineteenth century by getting himself declared Infallible. The Ode was written in one day in 1863, published in 1865, and again on the day of the opening of the Vatican Council. It is enough if it stood alone to disprove the notion of Carducci as mere academic

1   *The Catholic Encyclopaedia*, "Masonry (Freemasonry)", 1910

pedant. It sputters with fiery life from the first word to the last. But the Satan whom it proclaims and glorifies is not the spirit of evil; there is no less immoral poet than Carducci. His Satan is reason and nature, the body and the mind, all that revolts against the asceticism, sacerdotalism and obscurantism which have so often claimed to represent the Christian religion. The Hymn is as full of imagination as it is of spontaneity, sincerity, and strength. What it is not full of, either in thought or in language, is that grave music of the mind and of the word without which poetry cannot be entirely itself...Carducci's [*Hymn to Satan*] reads as little more than a piece of polemical journalism."[1]

Thereafter, Bailey went on to speak of what "is great and permanent" in the work of Carducci and to enumerate the many later poems and prose which did, indeed, in his opinion rise to the highest levels of the literary art and which were, of course, the basis of his winning the Nobel Prize. At the close of his lecture, Bailey concluded:

"The smith does not always succeed nor does the poet, each is clumsy sometimes and each sometimes finds his metal too hard to shape. What I have wished to say today is that Carducci succeeded often, and that when he succeeded it was with such materials, so finely worked, that his place among the poets is assured and immortal."

So, despite the revolutionary impact of Inno a Satana, Carducci's greatest poetic achievements still lay ahead. Carducci was a revolutionary on multiple fronts both political and artistic. Like his politics, Carducci's more advanced poetry became revolutionary as well. He was not afraid to undertake bold, daring adventures in his works. The Rime Nuove ("New Rhymes") and the Odi Barbare ("Barbaric Odes") which appeared in the 1880s contain the best of Carducci's poetry.

Odi Barbare in particular included brilliant, ground-breakng innovations. Carducci reintrocued old classical Latin poetry styles and meters into contemporary Italian-language works. This adaptation of ancient technique to new Italian recalled the pace and flavor of Homer and Virgil and was Carducci's way of honoring both classicism and paganism. It was also an attack upon two things he abhorred:

---

1   Bailey, John Cann, *Carducci - The Taylorian Lecture*, (Clarendon Press, Oxford) 1926.

the romanticism in contemporary poetry and the Christianity in contemporary society. Indeed, all of Carducci's work extolled Italian hope and Roman glory and was an assertion of classic reason as opposed to romantic mysticism and Roman Catholic piety.

He also wrote scathing reviews of what he considered trite sentimentalism in the gushing, unoriginal romantic poetry being churned out and lauded by his contemporaries.

These were all gutsy moves. To undertake such radical innovation in his own work and to so harshly criticize the popular Romantics, Carducci certainly showed he was willing to risk attracting condemnation that could hamper his popularity and his career. But, just as he had helped republican efforts to liberate Italian political life from royalist Hapsburg and Papal domination, Carducci also lead the liberation of Italian poetry from sentimental romanticism while at the same time offering it the innovation of his re-introduction of the meters of the classics. This was the cutting-edge artistry that brought him the Nobel.

When Carducci was selected to receive Nobel Prize in recognition of his worldwide acclaim, he was an old man and, indeed, was too ill to travel to Stockholm to accept the award in person. Had he been present, the Nobel committee might not have been so presumptuous as to try to make apologies for the great poet's "Satanism" or to attempt to separate him from Inno a Satana.

It is clear that even the relatively progressive intellectuals of the Nobel committee were uneasy with publicly embracing a pagan and Satanist like Carducci before a global audience. Their efforts to downplay these aspects of the man are evident in the presentation speech properly noting that his poetic brilliance transcended such things and (improperly) trying to show that he had disavowed/ retracted Inno a Satana.

While the whole of the Nobel presentation speech included the expected long laudatory recounting of the honored poet's life and accomplishments, it also included this tidbit of back-pedaling.

There is a good deal of justice in many of the attacks on Carducci's anti-Christianity. Although one cannot perfectly approve of the way in which he has tried to defend himself in Confessioni e Battaglie ("Confessions and Battles") and in other writings, knowledge of the attendant circumstances helps to explain, if not to justify, Carducci's attitudes.

Carducci's paganism is understandable to a Protestant, at least. As an ardent patriot who saw the Catholic Church as in many ways a misguided and corrupt force opposed to the freedom of his adored Italy, Carducci was quite likely to confuse Catholicism with Christianity, extending to Christianity the severe judgments with which he sometimes attacked the Church.

And as to the impetuous Inno a Satana, it would be a great wrong to Carducci to identify him, for example, with Baudelaire and to accuse Carducci of poisonous and unhealthy "Satanism." In fact, Carducci's Satan has an ill-chosen name. The poet clearly means to imply a Lucifer in the literal sense of the word—the carrier of light, the herald of free thought and culture, and the enemy of that ascetic discipline which rejects or disparages natural rights. Yet it seems strange to hear Savanarola praised in a poem in which asceticism is condemned. The whole of the hymn abounds with such contradictions. Carducci himself in recent times has rejected the entire poem and has called it a "vulgar sing-song." Thus, there is no reason to dwell any longer on a poem which the poet himself has disavowed.[1]

Their little fig leaf probably fooled no one for it was obvious that the master poet Carducci looked back to the dinner-table political toast of the early days of his art with a condemning eye only in assessing the poem's lack of artistic sophistication. Calling the poem "vulgar sing-song" was merely a repudiation of its youthful, immature poetic style. In his professional work, having introduced immense contributions to the field of poetry, he had long since moved beyond the silly, elementary structure of the provocative little rhyme he shared with friends and compatriots over a raised wine glass. But such self-criticism of that early work certainly did not imply any rejection of the substance of the sentiments expressed therein. Those he held to without apology to the very end of his days.

The Carducci monument in Bologna, Italy "I know neither truth of God nor peace with the Vatican or any priests. They are the real and unaltering enemies of Italy." he said in his later years.[2]

At the end of Carducci's life, Romanticism, Catholicism and (one could argue) political domination remained quite popular with the great mass of Italians, but his daring stabs at all three had unforgettably opened the door for the elite few seeking to liberate themselves politically, artistically and religiously. His lasting contribution to freedom of the mind and spirit is forever immortalized in the roster of the Nobel Prize, the highest literary distinction on Earth; in a beautiful stone monument in Bologna; in the pages of his still-

1   Nobel Lectures, *Nobel Prize for Literature 1906* - Presentation Speech
2   Carelle, *Naturalismo Italiano*

acclaimed works, and in the hearts of all that they still touch. And really, how much more immortality can any successful Satanist hope for than that?

R. Merciless
Washington, D.C.

THE POETRY OF CARDUCCI

When men are engaged in a long struggle for liberty they are apt to allow political prejudices to colour all their judgments, as Italian literature during the last century discovered to its cost. It is perhaps true to say that no Italian poet, from Alfieri to Carducci, has escaped criticism, which, however much it claim to be purely literary in character, is not in reality strongly influenced by political or religious considerations. In Carducci's case it has already been shown how his political evolution affected at once his own development as a poet and the attitude of his public. Now that he is dead, and the events about which he wrote are already passing into history, it should be easier for the critics to approach their task in a more dispassionate spirit, and endeavour to discover what lasting merits the *Poesia Carducciana*, as poetry pure and simple, really possesses.

Carducci himself recognised, as we have seen, that much of his work, especially his earlier political poetry, was only ephemeral. Yet, on the other hand, several of his poems "Ii Bove," "Pianto Antico," the Roman Ode, and some dozen others—have already won a permanent place in anthologies; and his admirers claim that the vast mass of his later poetry, represented by the *Rime Nuove*, the *Odi Barbare*, and the *Rime e Ritmi*, is destined to form an imperishable part of his country's literature.[1] Nor can it be denied that, from one point of view at any rate, these confident predictions will prove correct. As a political poet, and as the inventor of a new type of verse, Carducci will undoubtedly always secure for himself the attention of the historian and literary student of the future. Professor Benedetto Croce has, indeed, already distinguished two periods in modern Italian literature, the first extending from 1865 to 1885, and the second from 1885 or 1890 to the present day.[2] To the earlier of these periods he gives the name Carduccian, the later he calls that of D'Annunzio, Fogazzaro, and Pascoli. In these three poets and their age he discovers the greater finesse and intellectual subtlety; while to Carducci, on the other hand, he attributes the grand quality of sincerity. A man, then, who is big

---

1   *E.g.* Mazzoni says: "L'eternità d'amore risplenderà su lui finale la sua poesia sari sentita, ammirata, amata; e sari, finchè la lingua di Dante duri strumento di tutto quanto it pensiero e di tutto quanto it sentimento del popolo nostro, dalle Alpi alla Sicilia" (cp. Chian, *Mem.* p. 431).

2   Cp. B. Croce's *Letteratura e critica dell Letteratura contemporanea in Italia. Due saggi*, p. 11.

enough to dominate his country's literature for nearly a quarter of a century, who if he did not, like Manzoni, found a school, is at least the father in the Muses of many poets—among them two so eminent as Severino Ferrari and Giovanni Pascoli—whose historical odes are taught in all Italian schools, who earned for himself the title of 'Vate d'Italia' in the most supreme moments of modern Italian history, will assuredly never be forgotten. But whether his poetry will be read in the future for the sake of its own intrinsic merit is another question, and one which, to judge from the tone of some modern critics both in his own country and outside it, will not perhaps be answered in the affirmative quite so unanimously as the jealousy of his admirers would desire. An attempt, therefore, to discover the characteristic merits and failings of Carducci's verse may serve to help the reader to form his own opinion as to the poet's true greatness.

Carducci's importance in literature is due to the fact that he introduced a new ideal into Italian poetry. It is essential to define at the outset the nature of this ideal in order to avoid the error, committed by some critics, of blaming him for not performing something which he never set out to achieve. Carducci was one of the most outspoken of poets. He was provocatively frank both in his criticism of contemporary literature and in the statement of his own views. Caring nothing at all for public opinion, he never wrote to catch a public. "Let a poet express himself, his moral and artistic convictions, as sincerely, straightforwardly, and resolutely as he can: the rest is not then his affair."[1] Such was his attitude, and it should not be difficult to discover what these convictions were. They are summarised distinctly enough in a letter which he wrote at a time when his disgust with contemporary literature was at its height. After a very acute analysis of the genesis and the progress of Italian Romanticism, he defines the need of the present age in the following terms:—"We must make art realistic: represent what is real, in more natural terms, with truth. We must do away with the ideal, the metaphysical, and represent man, nature, reality, reason, liberty. To that end unite study of the ancients, who are realistic and free, Homer, Aeschylus, Dante, and of the popular poetry with modern sentiment and art."[2] If to this

---

1   Cp. *Critica ed Arte* (*Op.*, vol. iv. p. 285), where he quotes these words of his own.

2   *Lettere*, p. 143. "Bisogna fare l'arte realistica: rappresentare quel che è reale, in termini piú naturali, con la verità. Bisogna cacciar via l'ideale, il metafisico, e rappresentare l'uomo, la natura, la realtà, la ragione, la libertà. A ciò accoppiare lo studio degli antichi, che sono realistici e liberi, Omero, Eschilo, Dante, e della poesia popolare, col sentimento moderno

statement we add the first three verses of his brilliant lyric "The Poet" we shall obtain a sufficiently clear conception of what Carducci set before himself as the ideal poetic figure for his time.

> Il poeta, o vulgo sciocco
> Un pitocco
> Non è già, che a l' altrui mensa
> Via con lazzi turpi e matti
> Porta i piatti
> Ed il pan ruba in dispensa.
>
> E né meno a un perdigiorno
> Che va intorno
> Dando il capo ne' cantoni
> E co 'l naso sempre a l' aria
> Gli occhi varia
> Dietro gli angeli e i rondoni
>
> E né meno è un giardiniero
> Che il sentiero
> De la vita co 'l letame
> Utilizza, e cavolfiori
> Pe' signori
> E vïole ha per le dame.

It is obvious that, on its negative side, Carducci's diagnosis of the literary maladies of his age was defined by that hostility to the Italian Romantics. Because Romanticism indulged in the mystical and the vague, Carducci loved the real and the matter of fact; because the Romantic school was the school of the neo-Catholics and neo-Guelfs, Carducci stood for intellectual freedom and political independence; because Romanticism was attracted by the eccentric and abnormal, Carducci aimed at sanity of thought and strictness of form. But, on the positive side, Carducci's poetic ideal resulted quite logically from the nature of his own personal character, from his views on the relationship between poetry and politics, and from the fact that he possessed the true scholar's enthusiasm for classical literature.

---

e con l'arte." Cp. also the article "Di alcuni condizioni della presente letteratura" (*Op.*, vol. ii. p. 502), where he sums up the programme for a fresh departure in literature in the two words, "innoviamo rinnovando"— "Let our innovations be renovations.'

His was an essentially practical nature. He was never troubled with doubts or questionings about life, nor did the great problems of modern philosophy interest him at all. He was a Hellenist who, finding this world lovely and good to live in, did not concern himself about the next. He loved life for its own sake, and if in old age he is oppressed by melancholy at the thought of death, it is not the melancholy of Leopardi's "Shepherd of Asia," questioning the moon

> Che sia questo morir, questo supremo
> Scolorar del sembiante,
> E perir dalla terra, e venir meno
> Ad ogni usata, amante compagnia,

and yearning for an explanation of the secrets of the universe, but rather that of the Greek anthologist,

> Oh, tanto
> Breve la vita ed è si bello il mondo!

or of the cultured humanist, for whom the dark entrance to the unseen world is lit up by the calm radiance of Greek poetry:—

> A me prima che l'inverno stringa pur l'anima mia
> Il tuo riso, O sacra Luce, O divina poesia!
> Il tuo canto, O padre Omero
> Pria che l'ombra avvolgami.

Hence he turns with relief, if not with contempt, from the barren speculations of the metaphysicians and theologians. "The lazy fool, in hazy day-dreams rapt" is no true poet, or at least not the poet for modern Italy. What the country needed were men who, far from wasting time and energy over the "questions, the broods that haunt sensation insurgent," would employ all the resources of their imagination and insight in solving the practical problems of the national life.

When a nation is coming into existence, the most pressing problems that call for solution are political. So far from divorcing politics from poetry, it seemed to Carducci that the poet had a most necessary part to play on the political stage—a part, moreover, which none but he could play, and which could not be omitted without risk of disaster to the State. The poet, he maintained, when contented to pass with the public either for a *pitocco*, the servile minion of a patron or a party, or for a *giardiniero*, the writer of pretty but shallow, and possibly vulgar, society verse, is miserably failing in the duties of his own high calling. The nature of these duties may be deduced from Carducci's ideal picture of himself as his country's poet-seer. In *Critica ed Arte*, after dividing the history of poetry into clearly defined epochs, he thus describes the one at the close of which he himself was living: "And lastly there are other ages less glorious, in which, the nation being in a state of transition to new political conditions, the poets whom I will not by an archaism call true *vati* (seers), but who feel instinctively, like certain animals, a nervous uneasiness before the earthquake, begin transforming certain forms of art which are fully developed. These are the critical ages, when poets fight over their work with offensive and defensive weapons: and Alfieri writes the letter to Calsabigi, and Manzoni the letters on the dramatic unities and on Romanticism, and Victor Hugo the preface to Cromwell."[1] Here, then, he defines the poet-seer or *vate* as one who watches the times, who, by the exercise of a sense of intuition possessed by himself alone, perceives earlier than others the direction in which events are tending, and whose duty it is to warn and guide the nation in every crisis through which it may have to pass. It is the practical value of the imaginative faculty upon which Carducci here insists. The poet's function in his capacity of *vate* is moral. Himself anchored fast to some great guiding principle—in Carducci's case the ideal of a united Italy—he must, through good report or ill report, and without respect of person or of party, perform the office of inspired prophet of his people, expressing for them in outbursts of lyrical passion the emotions they feel but cannot utter, and equally prepared with warning or reproach whenever, through ignorance or blindness or pride, they seem to his clear sight in danger of falling short of their own highest ideals. For these reasons Carducci never feared the charge of being inconsistent in politics. The poet, as he rightly considered, has no concern with political consistency. "I intend, and have always intended, to express by a process of psychological purgation, with the greatest sincerity and efficacy possible, certain fancies and passions by which my spirit is moved, and to represent them exactly with the momentary shapes and colours in which I myself feel and see them, not with the shapes of yesterday, to-morrow, or some other day, and not with the shapes and colours in which other people wish to make me believe that other people will be better pleased to see them, or in

---

1   *Op.*, vol. iv. p. 278.

which other people may be able to see and feel something similar."[1] The poet, in fact, must be absolutely genuine, and if true to himself preserves a fundamental consistency that remains unaffected, however many times he may change sides in the conflict of political parties.

If personal characteristics and political enthusiasm were instrumental in shaping his poetic ideal, this was no less profoundly affected by his instincts as scholar and humanist. His innate hatred of the vague and superficial, not only in thought but in the realms of art and criticism, increased yearly in proportion as the true scholar's attention to accuracy and thoroughness of workmanship grew with him into a habit. The sense of clearly defined form, the lack of which he deplored in poets of the Romantic school, seemed to him to be an absolute essential of the great poet; and he held that it could only be learnt from the Greek. It was their power of treating romantic subjects with that great classical art which is of all time'[2] that caused him to place Goethe and Schiller so high above the German poets of their age. He himself was never tired of applying the principles of Greek art in the composition of his own verse, with the result that probably no poet that ever lived has composed so few slipshod lines or written his own language with greater purity of diction.

But he loved the classics not only for what they taught him about beauty of form. That beauty was to him only the outward and visible sign of the life and ideals of the ancient Greek world, to which he was as passionately devoted as the mediaeval humanist himself. "The ancients who are realistic and free"—by this he meant that, in contrast with the prevalent modern opinion, the old Greeks considered life to be something worth living for its own sake, not a mere vestibule of the world to come. Their thought was free because unfettered by dogmatic religions and unclouded by the vague abstractions of mysticism. Theirs was a concrete, not spiritual world, in which love was untinged by sentimentality, the virtues of the cloister unknown, and patriotic pride and manly vigour not yet superseded by the Christian qualities of resignation and humility. Into Carducci's ideal of poetry there entered, therefore, a very definitely pagan element. And herein he differs from other so-called classicists, who have earned the name merely in virtue of their allegiance to certain literary forms and conventions. Carducci wished to make the content of his poetry classical also, to regard both man and nature (so far as modern thought permitted) from the same point of view as the ancient Greek poets or as those Latin poets who

---

1   *Op. cit.*, p. 286.
2   *Lettere*, p. 140.

had modelled themselves on the Greek. By so doing he hoped to knit up again a literary tradition, which the Romantic movement in Italy had interrupted, but which he believed to be as distinctively native to his country as it was sanctioned by its antiquity and eternal youth. It was for these reasons that in his earlier work he employed every device of language and literary reminiscence, not excepting even literal translation, to reproduce as far as possible both the substance and the atmosphere of the Greek, Latin, and Italian classics; while in his later poetry he resorted more and more to his country's past, both in myth and history, as being the fittest of all possible subject-matter to inspire a patriot poet.

So much having been said, it becomes easier to understand why his poetic ideal took just the form it did. We shall expect to find him as a poet banishing from his verse all intellectual vapouring, meaningless abstractions, and vague emotionalism—suppressing, in fact, the subjective element[1] in poetry, as far as may be, altogether in order to concentrate his efforts on the objective presentation of life as it really is, in its beauty and ugliness, its joy and sorrow. If he is true to his own theories, we shall expect to find him pouring, as it were, the ancient Greek and Italian ideals into moulds of thought and language modelled, as closely as a sympathetic study of the classics can make them, upon those used by the ancient Greek and Italian poets. And, finally, we shall expect to find in him one who, by the true poet's gift of prophetic intuition, knows how to point his countrymen towards the glorious destiny that his ardent patriotism has imagined for them, while guiding, comforting, and exhorting them in their efforts to reach it.

If all this be summed up in his own words as the "representation of reality with truth," study of his poetry will reveal the fact that few men have more honestly put their own principles into practice. Carducci's conception of reality, considered from the artistic point of view, controls his treatment of all the chief themes of his poetry, as will at once become apparent if we examine any of these at all closely. Man, Nature, and Liberty, for instance—he held it incumbent upon

---

1   Carducci considered the most characteristic mark of Romanticism to be the exaltation of the *io*. Cp. *Op.*, vol. x. p. 286. "La nota piú sicura a cui riconoscere il romanticismo quale prevalse dal Rousseau in poi è, non la malinconia, non it ravvivamento del misticismo religioso piú o meno cristiano, non l'imitazione del medio evo e generalmente della poesia settentrionale, ma il predominio della personalità, dell' *io* indipendente da qualcosa piú the le regole e le consuetudini nella mutevole liberty delle impressioni e delle espressioni, l'esaltazione dell' *io*, la morbosità dell' *io*.'

the poets of his own time to deal mainly with these three, and they constitute accordingly a large portion of the subject-matter of his own verse. How are they treated according to the canons of Carduccian realism?

If we consider first the human element in his poems, it will be found that he eschews all abstract reasoning about mankind as such. Mankind, to Carducci, meant simply individual men and women. These men and women, moreover, are not creations of the poet's own brain, like Browning's "Cleon, Norbert, and the fifty." We find in Carducci's poetry no long reflective monologues, no dramatic lyrics, in which the inmost working of the human mind is revealed, and the hidden springs of action are traced to their source. On the contrary, it is the action itself, not the psychological dissection of the mind of the agent, which interests Carducci. Consequently the men and women that move across his pages are not there to illustrate his reading of human nature; they are not types but individuals, considered purely from the outside, objects of his respect, his hatred, or his admiration for something they have done or suffered in real life. They are, as already said, not created by his imagination at all, but contemporaries of himself or persons famous in political or literary history. Life, as lived in his own day or in past ages, teemed with poetic figures, ready to the poet's hand: men like Carlo Alberto, "the Italian Hamlet"; Garibaldi and Napoleon III; women like Marguerite of Savoy and Elizabeth, Empress of Austria. To be realistic, according to Carducci, is to take advantage of such historical figures as these, rather than to feed the fancy on the joys and sorrows of beings whom that fancy has itself created. Nor do the demands of realism end with the selection of subject; treatment must be realistic also. At this point Carducci the historian and Carducci the opponent of Romanticism join hands. No veil of romance must be spread by the poet over the personalities with which he deals. Imagination, which tends to idealise men out of all relation to humanity as it really exists, must be strictly controlled by historical fact Yet Carducci did not believe that a man, simply because historical, is of necessity a good subject for a poem. A man's career or character, to admit of poetic treatment, must be raised by some element of tragedy, beauty, or romance above those of the common herd. It is the duty of the poet as artist to isolate such figures in life or history as are suitable to his purpose from the *milieu* in which they occur, and then present them as graphically and truthfully as he can. For where the romantic element is a matter of historical fact, there is no need for the poet to invent it. On the other hand, it generally happens that the poet alone can disentangle that element from essentially prosaic ones by which it is obscured. Carducci therefore is realistic, because he insists that if the romance is not there the poet must not imagine it he is an idealist, in so far as he perceives that though facts be his subject-matter, his art must confine itself to those facts only which are in themselves instinct with poetry.[1] What such facts may be it is for the poet alone to say. A poem like "At the Station on an Autumn Morning" shows, at any rate, that Carducci, without falling away for an instant from his own high standard of poetic form, yet lacked none of the ability—which the modern realist is apt to consider peculiarly his own—to unearth poetry in apparently altogether prosaic material.

Carducci, then, felt that the more realistic, in the sense of truer to history, a poet shows himself to be, the greater will be the appeal of his poetry, just because it *is* true. And this was a consideration which in his character of poet-seer, with a moral function to perform, he could not afford to neglect. Consequently his men and women are not only historical characters, and hence obviously true from one point of view, but they are drawn with realistic touches either of person or setting, which serve to bring the man or the scene very vividly before us, and by their truth to fact and locality convince our reason at the same time as they stimulate our emotion. Take, for instance, the picture of Garibaldi retreating from Mentana:—

> Il dittatore, solo, a la lugubre
> Schiera d'avanti, ravvolto e tacito
> Cavalca: la terra e it cielo
> Squallidi, plumbei, freddi intorno.
>
> Del suo cavallo la pésta udivasi
> Guazzar nel fango: dietro s'udivano
> Passi in cadenza e sospiri
> De' petti eroici ne la notte.[2]

This is realistic, and it is poetry. The poetry consists in the historical truth of the picture, both subject and treatment. Garibaldi, the hero of the nation: fighting to win Rome, the ideal of the nation: retiring

---

1   Cp. Arist., *De art. poet.*, ix. 9. "Even if he (the poet) chances to take a historical subject, he is none the less a poet; for there is no reason why some events that have actually happened should not conform to the law of the probable or possible, and in virtue of that quality in them he is their poet or maker" (Butcher's translation).

2   Cp. p. 220.

defeated because unsupported by the Government of the nation! Here is no figment of the poet's brain but a tragic fact. The poem focuses and embodies for all time the storm of outraged patriotism which swept over Italy after the battle of Mentana. The realism of Carducci's descriptive touches intensifies but does not create the tragedy.

Again, to quote the last two matchless verses of the Alcaic ode[1] on the death of the Prince Imperial:—

> Sta nella notte la còrsa Niobe
> Sta sulla porta donde al battesimo
> Le usciano i figli, e le braccia
> Fiera tende su 'l selvaggio mare:
>
> E chiama, chiama, se da l'Americhe,
> Se di Britannia, se da l'arsa Africa
> Alcun di sua tragica prole
> Spinto da morte le approdi in seno.

Does not the tragedy of this wonderful picture gain immensely in effect from the fact of its *historic* truth? The mother of the Napoleons mourning for her children! How much less poignant would have been the haunting pathos of that "chiama, chiama" had Letizia never lived but in the imagination of the poet, or had her offspring been just ordinary children and not Napoleons!

If this is what Carducci means by representing reality with truth in his treatment of humanity, we shall find a still clearer instance of his application of the same principle when he deals with Nature. He loved Nature; but for him the word had no abstract signification. He constructed no religion of Nature like Wordsworth or Meredith; he made no allegories about her like Shelley; he had not the naturalist's knowledge of her that Tennyson possessed. Nature for him meant primarily the country as opposed to the artificiality of the town— the mountains, the sea, the sky, and all the beautiful and familiar scenes of country life. But he does not describe the country in general. Never having travelled abroad, he identifies Nature with the Italian landscape; nor is it even the Italian landscape in general, but limited in much of his poetry to the scenery of the Maremma and the Versilia, in the midst of which he had been brought up, and which he loved to revisit. When in later life he took to spending his holidays in the Italian Dolomites, this district also comes in for its due share of

---

1   Cp. p. 216.

attention, though his descriptions of it lack the spontaneous charm that breathes from every verse of a poem like "Davanti San Guido."' The point, however, to be emphasised is that the country he paints in his poetry is always *real*. It actually exists apart from his imagination. Indeed, the accuracy of the descriptions in many of his poems—' "Piemonte," for instance—errs not infrequently on the side of being too photographic, and at times even smacks a little of the guide-book. But Carducci felt that the natural beauty of Italy, like the poetry of such a career as Garibaldi's, needs the adornment of no romantic colouring. His principle was to use his eyes, not to read into Nature what was not there, but to describe what he saw with exactness and sympathy. Just as the reader can never appreciate the true beauty of such a poem as Browning's "Englishman in Italy" except by visiting Sorrento and Amalfi, so he must have travelled in the Tuscan Maremma, walked through the Versilia, or wandered among the mountains round Cadore to realise how convincingly Carducci has caught and expressed the poetry of his native land. He tends to become conventional, however, the moment he attempts to describe what he has not seen. Thinking of Nature always as she appears in certain localities known to himself, he could not give verisimilitude to a purely ideal landscape.[1] What is particular and matter of fact in Nature appeals to him. He has been called Virgilian in his treatment of Nature, but he has none of Virgil's haunting sense of the mysterious power shadowed forth in natural phenomena. He is Virgilian only in his affection and reverence for simple country scenes and rustic pursuits. The figures of man and beast at work in the fields, illustrating what he so happily calls "La giustizia pia del lavoro,"[2] as opposed to the unnatural conditions under which labour is pursued in great cities, never fail to make instant appeal to his imagination. He loves, like Virgil, to sing

> Wheat and woodland,
> Tilth and vineyard, hive and horse and herd.

Over and over again his poems bear convincing testimony to the intimate sympathy he felt with all the homely details of the peasant's life. Characteristic scenes and incidents of the Italian countryside are

---

1   This accounts for the literary atmosphere of the Sicilian landscapes in the "Primavere Helleniche" (Dorica) (cp. p. 156), which is comparable to the literary landscape of Tennyson's "Lotus-Eaters" or Virgil's *Eclogues*. Had Carducci visited Sicily we should have had something much more realistic.

2   In "La Madre" (cp. p. 238).

drawn with such a sure and vivid touch that even a single line or phrase frequently contains a complete picture; while the moral symbolism of toiling cattle or changing season is expressed (as in "Il bove" and "Canto di Marzo") with a grave simplicity and power, which recall Millet in painting, but to which it would be hard to find a parallel in the whole range of modern poetry.

It is interesting, further, to observe how characteristically Carducci's attitude towards Nature is affected by his patriotism. Many of his finest descriptions of Italian scenery occur in poems dealing with historical events and personages. He does not, however, simply make use of landscape as the *cadre* or setting for the historical and literary associations which must of necessity attach themselves to almost every square yard of an ancient country like Italy, and which it was his special delight, as a historian and archaeologist, to discover. His love of Nature and his love of history are really only two different manifestations of a deeper emotion still, his love of country; and patriotism enables him to combine the two in the description of a *paessaggio storico* in such a way as to give equal effect to both. Thus in the historical ode "Cadore"[1] the poet's patriotism forms an emotional bond between the beauty of the mountain scenery and the heroism of Pietro Calvi's deed. Pelmo and Antelao are pictured as sympathising with the band of patriots fighting below them. For the mountains *are* Italy, and Pietro Calvi was fighting for Italy; and it is because Carducci loves Italy that not only the natural beauty but the historical associations of "Cadore" appeal to him so forcibly. Consequently it is in deference to no mere literary convention that Carducci is led to personify Italy. He feels that she really is his mother, and he adores her with a filial affection. It is she who has given him, as she gave them to Dante before him,

> L'abito fiero e lo sdegnoso canto
> E il petto ov' odio e amor mai non s'addorme.

She is the bond that unites all the many nations that have ever called themselves Italian; all the poets who have ever sung her praises; all the patriots who "for her sake have fallen"; all those "who for her sake shall live." His love for her makes it easy and natural for him to pass from describing her beauty, as seen in mountain, stream, and sky, to reminiscence of her people and her history. He visits Sirmio,[2]

---

1   Translated, p. 198.
2   Cp. p. 212.

for instance, and the peninsula suggests memories of Catullus, Virgil, and. Dante; they are indeed historically connected with the locality, but Carducci's interest in the place is not merely archaeological. The real link between the three poets and himself is the common affection which all have cherished for "Italia Bella," "Italia madre." Sirmio, with its lovely scenery, is the. outward and visible object by which this common affection is symbolised, and as such has a message for the poet which the archaeologist would have missed.

The best example of this intermingling of Nature-description and historical reminiscence is afforded by the "Alle fonti di Clitumno,"[1] one of the most characteristically Carduccian (for this reason) of all Carducci's poems. He there exclaims:—

> A piè de i monti e de le querce a l'ombra
> Co' fiumi, O Italia, è de' tuoi carmi il fonte.

Carducci believed this with his whole soul, just because his intense patriotism saw in mountains, trees, and rivers not merely beautiful natural objects but his Mother Italy; and to him they were doubly a source of poetry, since besides their own intrinsic loveliness he looked upon them as links with the Past, beings whom he could compel by sheer force of learned imagination to speak to him of all the wonderful events of which they had been witnesses.

Turning now to Carducci's treatment of Liberty, a theme which for a hundred years had more than any other inspired Italians to be poets, we shall find him as careful as ever not to lose touch with concrete reality.

Of all his earlier poetry Liberty may be said to have been the dominating theme. It never ceased to be one of his main sources of inspiration. But if we are to call him a poet of Liberty, we must use the title in a very different sense to that in which he himself conferred it upon Shelley. The author of the *Prometheus Unbound* pursues Liberty as an abstract ideal, fashioned after a pattern laid up in heaven, and only dreams of it as wholly realisable in some paradise of the poet's imagination. Such a Platonic conception as this Carducci would have speedily banished "tra le fantasmagorie di un mondo impossibile." It partook far too much of the romantic and mystical; whereas his own ideal of the free citizen in the free state presented a practical end, clearly conceived and capable of very definite statement. That practical end was neither the liberation of the human soul nor of the

---

1   Cp. p. 204.

world in general, but the freedom of Italy. As an ideal to be fought for, it calls up visions of the battles and heroes of the Risorgimento, of Pisacane, the brothers Cairoli, and above all, Garibaldi; as an ideal to be realised, it simply means the Tricolour flying over Rome. Not until Rome is free and the Papacy overthrown does his conception of Liberty at all widen its scope; and the poet, with the history of ancient Rome in his mind, dreams of a time when the capital of united Italy shall once more become the central source of all principles of freedom and justice throughout the world.[1]

> E tu dal colle fatal pe' l tacito
> Fero le braccia porgi marmoree,
> A la figlia liberatrice
> Additando le colonne e gli archi:
>
> Gil archi che nuovi trionfi aspettano
> Non piú di regi, non piú di Cesari,
> E non di catene attorcenti
> Braccia umane su gli eburnei carri;
>
> Ma il tuo trionfo, popol d'Italia,
> Su l'età nera, su l'età barbara,
> Su i mostri onde tu con serena
> Giustizia farai franche le genti.
>
> O Italia, O Roma! quel giorno placido
> Toners it cielo su 'l Fòro, e cantici
> Di gloria, di gloria, di gloria
> Correran per l'infinito azzuro.[2]

Enough has perhaps been said to enable the reader to grasp the chief

---

1   Cp. *Op.*, vol. i. p. 23 ("Lo Studio di Bologna"). "Oggi che l'Italia per virtú del suo lungo martirio, ha inaugurato l'età nuova degli stati nazionali, perché non potrebbe chiamar questa età a ricevere ne' nuovi ideali politici, dei quali irrequietamente ella va in traccia, quanto del diritto pubblico romano non fu di dispotismo imperiale? L'Italia nella poesia, nell' arte, nella filosofia fece rivivere all' Europa le idee dell' antichità piú serena delle razze ariane, idee d'armonia, d'ordine, di bellezza, con tale un' efficacia di bene, che è lungi dall' essere indebolita. Perché da quella Roma che seppe cost gloriosamente riunire le genti non potrebbe l'Italia dedurre ancora i principii che informino e reggano le nuove nazioni e la loco federazione spontanea?"

2   Translated, p. 149.

themes of Carducci's poetry, together with the point of view from which he treats them. It was obviously impossible for him, holding the opinions he did, to be a love-poet in the ordinary sense of the term. Much of modern love-poetry is essentially romantic. It springs from the idealisation of woman. The lover endows his mistress, whether she possesses them or not, with every imaginable grace and virtue, and sets her on a pedestal, from which, like a deity, she is permitted to influence his life for good or bad. Carducci, as Professor Croce has pointed out,[1] removes Love from this central position in life; and he does so by rehumanising woman. He brings her down from her pedestal, and transforms her again into a creature of flesh and blood. With a healthy naturalism which is never coarse, he loves, like Walt Whitman, to dwell upon the mere physical attractiveness of a beautiful woman.

He does not care for ethereal types of female loveliness. The latter, to appeal to him, must be combined with health and strength, because every young girl is potentially a wife and mother, and it is in the due performance of her functions in both these capacities that Carducci finds the truest poetry of womanhood. Thus in the "Idillio Maremmano"[2] he plunges into no sentimental rhapsodies about "la bionda Maria," whom he had once loved, but merely gives us a realistic sketch of a young *contadina* crossing the cornfields on a summer afternoon—a girl whose vigorous personal charms, he thinks, must surely very soon have secured for her the joy of husband and children:—

> Ché il fianco baldanzoso ed il restio
> Seno a i freni del vel promettean troppa
> Gioia d'amplessi al marital desio.
> Forti figli pendean da la tua poppa
> Certo, ed or baldi un tuo sguardo cercando
> Al mal domo caval saltano in groppa.

Again, his poem "La Madre,"[3] one of the most beautiful he ever wrote, paints for us the picture of healthy human motherhood as opposed to the *disutili amori* with which Romanticism loves to coquet.

What, then, is to be said of the Lalages, Lidias, and other ladies with Greek names to whom he addresses so many of his later odes

---

1   In *La Critica*, vol. viii. (1910), p. 89.
2   Cp. p. 166.
3   Cp. *infra*, p. 236.

and elegies? We have only to compare any one of these with the "Maria" of the "Idillio Maremmano" to perceive that there is in them no more substance than the literary flavour of their names is intended to suggest. They only serve, in fact, as part of the conventional furniture of poems written on classical models. The real motive to lyrical passion in these cases must be sought, not in the poet's love for Lalage or Lidia, but in Patriotism, Liberty, or the purely literary enthusiasm of an ardent Hellenist.[1] The beautiful "Primavere Helleniche," for instance, addressed to Lina, are not love-poems. They only seek, like Alma Tadema's pictures, to reproduce artistically the idyllic charm of ancient Greek life. Their interest is aesthetic and literary, not personal. The same holds true of Lidia in "In a Gothic Cathedral,"[2] and of Lalage in "By the Urn of P. B. Shelley"[3]—in both of which lyrics the writer appears primarily as Hellenist, not lover. Even the Alcaic ode entitled "At the Station on an Autumn Morning,"[4] where personal affection for Lidia seems to play a more important part, is chiefly interesting as a specimen of modern impressionism cast in an ancient classical verse form. Of love-poems proper Carducci wrote none.[5]

This purely artistic use of women's names in his poetry suggests the consideration of Carducci as literary craftsman. From this point of view he himself invented the figure which most aptly describes him when he pictures the poet as a mighty smith,[6] who hammers into beautiful shapes "the elements of Thought and Love, and the memories and glories of his fathers and his nation." It is as a master of style and of metrical composition that Carducci, as some believe, is destined to live longest. "Carducci," says Dr. Garnett, "has solved the problem which baffled the Renaissance, of linking strength of

---

1   Cp. Card., *Lettere*, p. 181. "…di quando in quando bisogna concedermi questi ritorni alla contemplazione serena o quasi idolatrica delle pure forme estetiche della Grecia naturalmente divina: di quando in quando bisogna concedermi the io mi riposi in questi *lavori di cesello*, che mi vi distragga della realtà, la quale finirebbe per soffocarmi nello sdegno e nel fastidio.'

2   p. 156.

3   p. 178.

4   p. 169.

5   Unless a poem like "Ad Annie" (*Poesie*, p. 957) be considered a love-poem. It is addressed to Signorina Annie Vivanti, whose poems and plays he reviewed (cp. *Op.*, vol. x. p. 279), and with whom he corresponded (*Op.*, vol. xi. p. 353). He certainly seemed to have entertained for her a feeling of admiration, amounting to something more than mere friendship.

6   *Vide* his poem "Il Poeta," p. 141.

thought to artifice of form."[1] The secret of his style, a secret he wrung from the great classical poets after years of loving study, consists in its restrained power and in the precision of its artistic finish. Metaphors from sculpture naturally suggest themselves to describe the massive and noble form in which all his most characteristic poems are cast. Like the statuary's, his art does not rely upon atmospheric charm or vague suggestiveness for securing its effects. He conceived some large and simple thought, and then endeavoured to achieve an equal breadth and simplicity in the form of its expression. His frequent success in accomplishing this is due partly, of course, to his stern practice of eliminating from the verse all words not absolutely essential. But strict economy in language would not in itself wholly account for the firm, smooth surface and clear-cut, definite outline attained by his best poems. These result from clearness and simplicity of thought combined with a complete mastery over his artistic medium—words. His confessed model was Horace, and there are abundant signs that he both studied and practised the precepts of the *Ars poetics*. What particularly attracted him to Horace was the inimitable and inevitable form into which the Augustan poet cast his thought. The Horatian *curiosa felicitas* is a striking characteristic of Carducci himself, and frequently defies translation. No servile imitation of his model, however, could have given him the power thus to manipulate language. It was because he shared with Horace a real love for words and their literary history that he became like him

In verbis etiam tenuis cautusque serendis.[2]

To compare him with D'Annunzio, the other great artist among modern Italian poets, is to illustrate by contrast Carducci's view concerning the proper function of language in poetry. The charm of D'Annunzio's style[3] is similar to that described and vindicated in Verlaine's poem "Art poetique":—

Il faut aussi que to n'ailles point
Choisir les mots sans quelque méprise:

---

1   Garnett, *Italian Literature*, p. 398.
2   Horace, *Ars poet.*, 1. 46.
3   Perhaps it would be fairer to say "one of D'Annunzio's styles," for he
      has many styles, and excels in all. Nevertheless, his love of language
      for its own sake and of the music of words, as apart altogether from the
      meaning they convey, is one of his most marked characteristics, wherein
      he resembles our own Swinburne.

Rien de plus cher que la chanson grise
Où l'Indécis au Précis se joint.

Car nous voulons la Nuance encore,
Pas la Couleur, rien que la nuance!
Oh! la nuance seule fiance
Le rêve au rove et la flûte au cor!

According to the view here advanced, the literal signification of the words he uses is among the least of a poet's concerns. What the words mean is not so important as the sensuous dreams their mere music and colour are intended to suggest. Conscious art in their selection is deprecated. It is the poet's task by the exercise of a sort of artistic instinct to weave word-magic out of a maze of subtle hints and delicate nuances, and so to create a mood rather than convey an idea. Even if Carducci had not been constitutionally opposed to all that is vague and indefinite, the very fact that he was a philologist as well as a poet would have prevented him from taking this view. He did not regard words as of value in themselves, symbols of emotional states which baffle precise expression, but as units of language, appealing primarily to the intellect, and each intended to possess some perfectly clear and definite connotation. They were the concrete material out of which the poem as a work of art was to be constructed, the means to an end, as is marble or bronze for the sculptor. Consequently Carducci's language is never difficult to understand. If it is obscure, the obscurity arises from over-compression, not because the thought is slovenly or because the poet is seeking to achieve a general emotional effect at the expense of logic.

His profound knowledge of both ancient and modern literature naturally affects his style. He was particularly fond of insisting on the unbroken linguistic ties connecting the Latin and Italian languages. Nothing delights him more than to surprise the reader with cadences and phrases definitely recalling passages of Horace and other Latin poets; nor, if occasion demands, does he hesitate to coin words direct from the Latin in proof of the close kinship still existing between the two tongues. For a similar reason it interested him to imitate old Italian verse forms, and sometimes to reinstate words which had fallen into disuse. All this gives a distinctly literary atmosphere to his poetry, which, if it delights some readers for this very reason, will as inevitably fret others who cannot command one tithe of the vast learning which the poet himself had amassed. To quote his own simile, he hammered his verse with immense care, and very few of his best poems give the impression of having been written down hurriedly under the stress of an overmastering inspiration. The "Hymn to Satan" was indeed composed in a single night, and many of the *Iambics and Epodes* were evidently thrown off in moments of intense emotion. But for the most part, at any rate in later life, he preferred to concentrate thought and feeling into few but telling words, rather than to let them carry him away in a torrent of passionate eloquence. The elaborated intensity of his descriptive word-painting is the outward sign of the conscious art with which he worked; nor could any poet have evolved the metres of the *Barbarian Odes* without spending years of labour on problems of metrical technique.

From what has now been said about Carducci's temperament and theories on poetry may be divined the kind of faults to which as a poet he is most liable. These perhaps will be best brought out by a glance at the criticism which his work as a whole has excited. Apart from the abuse of political opponents, who would have liked him to remain for ever as he was when he wrote the *Iambics and Epodes*, the general complaint of his critics may be summed up in the statement that he ought not really to be called a poet at all in the strict sense of the word, but that he is rather a professor exceptionally skilled in the art of versification. This criticism, serious enough if well-founded, is stated by different critics in various forms. Thus his French biographer, M. Jeanroy, in a final summary of Carducci's whole literary output, remarks: "Le verbe, grâce à sa profonde culture d'humaniste, était plus riche que l'imagination."[1] He had too many models, and he reproduced them too faithfully. He is too classical, says another critic, and not sufficiently original; woman, the eternal theme of all poetry, he hardly touches on.[2] Fortibracci drew attention to the fact that an event or landscape rarely inspires him for its own sake. The event recalls to his memory other historical records, the landscape reminds him of passages in the poets.[3] Enrico Thovez, himself a poet and one of Carducci's acutest critics, in contrasting the latter's *Barbarian Odes* with the *Canti* of Leopardi, complains that "he hastened to clothe the psychological immodesty of that nakedness [Leopardi's] with rich verbal ornaments fished up from the Greeks and Latins, from the *dugentisti* and *trecentisti*, from the fourteenth and fifteenth century. He indulged in an orgy of literary phraseology, characteristic

1   A. Jeanroy, G. Carducci, *l'homme et le poète*, p. 257.
2   A. Oriani; so quoted by B. Croce in *La Critica*, vol. viii. p. 4.
3   *Gazzetta letteraria di Milano-Torino*, quoted by Croce (*op. cit.*).

of professors who write poetry. Just as the substance of his poetry was archaic and historical, so was its medium of expression archaic and historical. He sought by every device to banish every trace of plain, living, contemporary reality. What was the reason of this hatred of present reality—that is, of living Nature? The reason is simple enough: Carducci's inner world was not life, it was a literary organism."[1] Even Chiarini, his bosom friend and enthusiastic biographer, admits that the difficulties experienced by many highly cultured men in first reading his poetry arose from the fact that every line was "so packed with thought and saturated with learning."[2]

This is not the place to attempt any detailed defence of Carducci against his critics. Every poet, sooner or later, has to pass through a period of depreciation, which must, in his own interest, be allowed to run its course. And certainly Carducci himself, with his characteristic contempt for "i pappagalli lusingatori," would have been the last man to shrink from honest criticism. Moreover, it would be idle to deny that there is at least an element of truth in some of the charges brought against his poetry. It is at times, as Nencioni remarked in an otherwise enthusiastic appreciation of the "Ode to the Queen," "un po' faticosa, ricercata, quasi oscura."[3] The main contention of Thovez, however, that Carducci was no poet in the true sense of the word but only a professor writing verse, is obviously a superficial half-truth, based on an absurdly narrow definition of what constitutes poetry. Let it be freely admitted that Carducci had the defects of his own virtues. It is indeed obvious that from a man of his enormous culture, a professor constantly engaged in lecturing and research work, a scholar among scholars, we can hardly expect the native wood-notes wild of an untaught bard of Nature. Examples of tiresome pedantry and of learning unnecessarily paraded may be culled, no doubt, from Carducci's verse, as they may be from that of even so great a poet as Milton. Milton's *Lycidas*—not to mention the *Paradise Lost*—smacks of the scholar's study, if any poem ever did,[4] and contains references

1   E. Thovez, *Il Pastore, il Gregge e la Zampogna*, p. 70.
2   "Le poesie del Carducci in generale, e le *Odi Barbare* in particolare vogliono essere lette con molta attenzione nel silenzio tranquillo del proprio studio: vogliono, dirò di più, essere meditate e studiate, come tutta la poesia densa di pensiero e nutrita di dottrina: senza di ciò è impresa disperata it comprenderle" (*Mem.* p. 381).
3   Cp. the review *Acropoli*, vols. vi.-vii. p. 487. Nencioni is here quoted by M. Pelaez in his article on Chiarini's metrical versions of Horace.
4   Edward FitzGerald says of Milton's poetry in one of his letters: "I never could read ten lines together without stumbling on some pedantry that tipped me at once out of Paradise, or even Hell, into the schoolroom,

which would be unintelligible to the average reader without the assistance of notes. Yet *Lycidas* remains a great poem, and that, too, not in spite of, but because of, its essentially literary charm; and the same may be said of Carducci's Roman Ode, which only a scholar could have written, which perhaps only a scholar can fully appreciate, as well as a score of the other great *Barbarian Odes*. Moreover, it is not necessarily a reproach to a poet that he imitates other poets. Criticism rarely enters upon a more perilous, certainly never upon a more unworthy, enterprise than when it endeavours to undermine a great poet's reputation by denying him originality. Carducci's debt to Heine and Victor Hugo and other contemporaries was no doubt a heavy one. He acknowledged it himself. Equally obvious was his conscious imitation of the classics. But this in itself affords no proof that he could only write poetry at second-hand. The whole question of plagiarism—what constitutes it, and to what extent it is justified—is often misconceived. In one sense all great poets are, and perhaps must be, plagiarists.[1] Goethe once remarked to Eckermann "Shakespeare ist für aufkeimende Talente gefährlich zu lesen: er nötigt sie, ihn zu reproduciren, and sie bilden sich ein, sich selbst zu reproduciren." Substitute Horace for Shakespeare and the truth of this dictum might be well illustrated from Carducci's *Juvenilia*. If he had written only the *Juvenilia* those critics who assert that his world was not life but literature would be probably stating little less than the truth, though even then such a stricture could not be accepted without qualification. But it need hardly be pointed out that the instances of imitation in Carducci's later poetry—that is, in all poems written after the *Iambics and Epodes*—must be judged from a new and different standpoint, the justification of which may again be explained by a reference to Goethe. When the latter was asked why he had incorporated a song from Shakespeare's *Hamlet* without alteration into his own *Faust*, he replied: "Why should I give myself the trouble to invent a song of my own when Shakespeare's was just right and said precisely what was wanted?"[2] From a similar motive Carducci, no doubt, deliberately imitated Heine, simply because Heine so exactly expressed his own

---

worse than either."

1   To borrow or steal from other poets without acknowledgment is, of course, *morally* very reprehensible. From the *artistic* point of view, however, it is no crime, so long as what is borrowed fits in perfectly with its new context. If it does so, the new context gives it new interest, and the plagiarism is artistically justified. It is in this sense that all great artists are plagiarists.

2   Cp. Eckermann, *Gespräche mit Goethe*, Leipzig, 1909 (Houben), p. 111.

sentiments. "It is impossible," says Shelley in the Introduction to his *Prometheus*, "that any one who inhabits the same age with such writers as those who stand in the foremost ranks of our own can conscientiously assure himself that his language and tone of thought may not have been modified by the study of the productions of those extraordinary intellects." Since, therefore, Carducci desired to be to Italy what Heine and Hugo had been to Germany and France, it was both natural and justifiable that he should imitate, and even deliberately imitate, these two great poets closely. In fact, granted that he was a student of their works, the real affectation would have consisted in not doing so. If it is easy to trace verbal imitations of others in Carducci, that is only because he was great enough not to need, and honest enough not to try, to conceal his obligations.

Again, the air of artificiality about some of Carducci's poems admits of both a natural and reasonable explanation. It is the necessary accompaniment of his successful adaptation of the old Italian metres to modern poetry. Metrical experiments formed a necessary stage in the process by which Carducci's art was perfected. In these experiments the poet is bestowing, and we feel that he is bestowing, more attention on the form than on the substance of the verse. But to assert that he never reached a time when he moved with perfect ease in these ancient metres, and made them just as suitable as rhyme for expressing modern ideas, is to deny all but an academic interest to a large body of masterpieces, of which even Thovez himself exclaims that they are "cose bellissime,"[1] and which in themselves are more than enough to place their author in the front rank of great European poets of the nineteenth century.

The truth is that the real quarrel which his critics have with Carducci is not that he is sometimes too rhetorical, too learned, too fond of invective—all of which no one need concern himself to deny—but that he is so rationalistic and humane, whereas they think that poetry must be something essentially subjective and sensuous rather than intellectual in its appeal. They find in Carducci no abandon of lyrical passion, no intense personal sympathy with the great elemental emotions of the human heart. Though the vast mass of his work is lyrical, yet the true lyric note, they complain, is wanting. Reason controls feeling at every step; conscious art gives an air of cold and studied correctness even to those national odes which he intended should glow with the fire of his own passionate patriotism. In the supreme poetic product of this self-styled "Vate d'Italia," his *Barbarian Odes*, they find neither the

---

1   Cp. *Il Pastore, il Gregge e la Zampogna*, p. 79.

"heat of pale-mouthed prophet dreaming" nor

> The immortal thought,
> Whose passion still
> Makes of the changing
> The unchangeable.

In short, Carducci's poetry, greatly as it excites their admiration in virtue of its formal beauties, yet leaves their souls untouched.

Now, even admitting all that these critics complain of to be true—and of its truth the public, not the critics, are after all the only reliable judge—yet nothing more is proved thereby than that Carducci's poetry does not fit in with their preconceived notions of what poetry ought to be. It is as absurd to contrast Dante or Leopardi with Carducci, to the disparagement of the latter, as it would be to condemn Horace for his inability to write the *Æneid* of Virgil or to compose love-lyrics in the manner of Catullus. Any definition of poetry to justify itself should be wide enough to include all types. Nor can hard and fast lines be drawn between different types. If Horace chose to confine himself to didactic verse, his rhetoric was capable of rising to the height of really great poetry when dealing with such a theme as, say, the departure of Regulus from Rome. Although Carducci chose to make his poetry impersonal and objective, he could none the less write, under the stress of strong personal emotion, such cries from the heart as "Pianto antico" and "The Guide's Funeral." He cannot be called, it is true, a poet of the human soul, although this does not mean that he was incapable of appreciating the greatness of such a poet. In one of his many learned contributions to the study of Dante he discovers the secret of the great Florentine's appeal to successive ages in the fact that he is a singer ` of the deepest things in life, the deepest thoughts of men, the deepest secrets of the soul, not of his own soul only, but of all souls.'[1] To greatness of this kind, however, Carducci laid no claim. Insight into the deepest mysteries of divine and human nature, the joys and sorrows of the spiritual life, he neither possessed nor cared to possess. Critics, therefore, who deplore his limitations in this respect are drawing attention to a fact which may be regrettable perhaps, but carries us no further than that Carducci is not so great a poet as Dante, and not the same kind of poet as, let us say, Leopardi or Robert Browning—a conclusion so obvious that it is hardly worth stating. What Carducci might have achieved had his sympathy with

---

1   *L'Opera di Dante* (*Op.*, vol. i. p. 236).

Christianity been equal to his hatred of Roman Catholicism, it is idle to speculate. A Christian Carducci, or a philosophical Carducci, might have appealed to a larger public and to a more distant posterity, but would certainly not have accomplished the task set himself by the pagan Carducci. In the accomplishment of this task he deemed it necessary to exclude from his verse many of those very qualities which his critics blame him for not cultivating, as well as to include others they dislike. To repress all merely personal emotion, consciously to control both the substance and form of his poetry by reason, was precisely the end at which he aimed, because he believed that thus alone could he counteract certain unhealthy tendencies in contemporary literature, and at the same time most sincerely express the best both in himself and his age. It may be admitted that his hatred for Romanticism—a hatred arising, as we have shown, by no means entirely from literary causes—made him unnecessarily narrow in his ideals and stunted his genius on one side of its development. Yet he was undoubtedly right in his contention that there are certain characteristics of the Romantics, such as the "love of vivid colouring and strongly marked contrasts, the craving for the unfamiliar, the marvellous, the supernatural,"[1] which when transplanted from their native home in the colder north, and allowed to take root as exotics beneath the warmth of "Latin suns," tend naturally to spring up too rapidly, only then to get out of control and work havoc with the classical traditions of Italian literature. The Italian nature, so open to sensuous appeal, and with passions naturally so near the surface, stands in special need of the controlling force of reason. The Italian language, unless submitted to the strictest formal restraint, degenerates only too quickly into mere fluent prettiness. The way in which Carducci's own noble Hellenism, reproducing so faithfully the highest ideals, both moral and artistic, of ancient Greece, has been debased by D'Annunzio and his imitators to a decadent æstheticism "sweet - smelling, pale with poison" is proof enough that the instinct which bade Carducci as a poet trust to reason rather than feeling was perfectly sound. "Alla fin," he said, to quote his own picturesque epigram, "Manzoni trae la gente in sacrestia, il Byron in galera, it Leopardi al ospedale"[2]; and he might have added, "il D'Annunzio al bordello."

Carducci's critics would be more convincing, therefore, if they could show that their case against him is not based, as it seems to be, on a too narrow definition of what constitutes poetry, or that the

---

1   Vaughan, *The Romantic Revolt*, p. 3.
2   *Op.*, vol. xii. p. 499.

undesirable tendencies in Italian literature, against which he sought to create a reaction, either did not exist or, if they did exist, might have been checked by means other than those which he actually employed. If they adopt the latter course they will hardly find the average productions of the Manzonian school very promising material with which to illustrate their argument. Meanwhile his admirers are content to believe that Carducci's transparent sincerity, his Hellenic devotion to severe yet flexible beauty of form, his indifference to what is complex and subtle, his hatred of mere fluent emotionalism, combined with the ability to express deeply felt passions with the most rigorous self-restraint, and, finally, his intense loyalty to the ancient classical traditions of Italian poetry, provided not only the very antidote required against the unhealthy influences of an outworn Romantic school, but also responded, as nothing else could have done, to certain imperious demands of his own age. There have been ages which lacked their sacred bard, and there have been bards, potentially great poets, who lacked a sacred age to draw out their genius. Had Carducci been starting his career now he might perhaps have had to be included in the latter category. It is possible, or at least arguable, that Nature gave him greater powers of artistic expression than of creative imagination. If he had lived in the twentieth century he might only have ranked as one among a host of minor poets, who attain a high standard of technical ability in their art, yet fall short of true greatness for lack of a great theme. But Carducci was fortunate in the age into which he was born. No country can pass through a ' springtime more holy ' than that in which it is acquiring National Liberty and laying the foundations of National Unity. At such a time a nation does not need a great poet to dream great dreams for it. It dreams them of itself. It rather demands one who can express its great ideals for it and save it from forgetting them in the reaction which follows victory. To perform this double function Carducci's genius was admirably fitted. He possessed to the full the necessary sympathy which enabled him to identify himself with the national aspirations. He did not live apart from the world, hidden in the light of his own thought, but was first and foremost an Italian citizen and a very human man.[1]

> Son cittadino, per te d' Italia
> Per te poeta, madre de i popoli.

---

[1]   Cp. G. Pascoli, *Commem. di G. C. nella nativa Pietrasanta*, p.27. "Uomo! o cittadini di Pietrasanta, voi mi chiamasti a far l'apoteosi del vostro grande, e io non l'indiamento, si ye ne faccio piuttosto *l'umanamento*."

In these words he acknowledges the debt he owed to the age in which he lived, and above all to that unique city which, as the symbol of all that was greatest in Italian life and history, had inspired the inmost spirit of his poetry. And, secondly, his passion for classical models and his complete assimilation of their spirit enabled him, at the right time, to work upon the surging mass of national emotion, when it threatened to overflow its proper limits, in such a way as to separate by a process of strict formal isolation those elements in it which were good from those which were vicious. "There is an inevitable tendency," as Carducci himself remarked, "for a social order, which has brought about a revolution, to recuperate itself after the fasts and heroic self-denials of the struggle by bursting out into an exaltation of victory, power, and life. Then arises the danger lest, drunk with sensualism, it should defile the forms of art, pour out their contents in the gutter for rogues to drink and squander and dogs to lap."[1] How could a danger of this kind be more effectually met than by Carducci's poetry, with its noble submission to the strictest laws of form and its unwavering appeal to that which

> Dal Hutto de le cose emerge
> Sola, di luce a secoli affluenti
> Faro, l'Idea?

And so it is that Carducci's greatness seems due not only to what he said but even more to the way in which he said it. Whatever in his poetry makes him truly representative of his age—ideas such as Country, Patriotism, Liberty—would no doubt have found poetic expression for themselves somehow, even if Carducci had never lived. Wherever he admits the intrusion of his own purely personal views—on religion or politics, for instance—the necessary limitations of a man of his particular temperament and bringing up immediately betray themselves. What gives its distinctive value and quality to his work is its form. There exists a relationship between form and substance in art which Carducci was quick to perceive, and certainly intended his own verse to illustrate, as the following lines, prefixed to his *Barbarian Odes*, prove:—

Schlechten gestümperten Versen genügt ein geringer Gehalt schon,
  Während die edlere Form tiefe Gedanken bedarf:

---

1   *Op.*, vol. iv. p. 278.

Wollte man euer Geschwätz ausprägen zur sapphischen Ode,
  Würde die Welt einsehn, dass es ein leeres Geschwätz.[1]

These two couplets of Platen summarise Carducci's artistic creed, and suggest his view of the relation of poetry, as an art, to life. Nobility of form demands a corresponding nobility of content. The value of ideas may be tested in their formal expression. From the purely artistic point of view this means no more than that in all really great art form and substance must be so intimately bound up with one another as to be inseparable even in thought. But Carducci is also thinking of the relation of art to life. The life and ideals of a nation are indicated by the forms of its art. If its life be controlled by reason, so will its art be also. Similarly, by a reverse process, form will react on content, art upon life. "Es liegen," said Goethe, "in den verschiedenen poetischen Formen geheimnissvolle grosse Wirkungen." It is the privilege of the great artist to elevate, as it is in his power to debase, the ideals of his country-men. We have already referred to the moral implication involved in the title *vate* to which Carducci aspired. Realising that the restraint of Greek art resulted from the same controlling intellect as governed Greek life, and since restraint was the note he desired to introduce not only into the poetry, but through poetry into the ideals, of his own age, he deliberately adopted classical forms into Italian verse. By so doing he hoped to introduce the classical spirit also. Idealise Liberty in an Alcaic ode, he argued, and if the art be good—that is, if form and content correspond—the idea itself will of necessity assume the severe yet majestic proportions of the verse which expresses it. On the other hand, the qualities that belong to the sensuous language and loose or rhymed metres of modern poetry envelop the thought in an enervating atmosphere highly charged with emotion, which, be it good or bad, is apt sometimes to burst in a storm of passion beyond all the bounds of reason, and in any case favours the growth of an unwholesome æstheticism, ending often in undisguised sensuality.[2] "To our mind,"

---

1   "A mean content is enough for bad bungling verses, whereas the nobler form needs profound thoughts. Were your idle chatter to be stamped into a Sapphic ode, the world would perceive its emptiness."

2   Cp. *Op.*, vol. xi. p. 237. (Preface to *Od. Barb.*) "La lirica . . . pub durare ancora qualque poco, a condizione per altro che si serbi arte: se ella si riduce ad essere la secrezione della sensibilità o della sensualità del tale e del tale altro, se ella si abbandona a tutte le rilassatezze e le licenze innaturali che la sensibilità e la sensualità si concedono, allora, povera lirica, anche lei la vedo e non la vedo." Cp. also his attack on "Poetry of the Heart" in *Intermezzo*.

says Carlyle somewhere of Goethe's *Helene*, "there is everywhere a strange, piquant, quite peculiar charm in these imitations of the whole Greek style…often so graphic in the delineation we could almost feel as if a vista were opened through the long gloomy distance of the ages, and we with our modern eyes and modern levity beheld afar off in clear light the very figures of that grave old time." "Modern levity," which tends to "debase the forms of art," was the foe against which Carducci fought. As a spiritual descendant of Goethe, he fought it with weapons from the Olympian's armoury, only using the lyric instead of the drama. He did not, however, try to make the present fit the past, as initiators of classical reactions have sometimes done, seeking to impose the outworn forms of "a grave old time" upon new material unfitted to receive them. On the contrary, he forced the past to acknowledge its oneness with the present by endeavouring to show that the same principles of formal beauty which had produced the *antichità serena* of old Greece and Rome were still those in obedience to which modern Italy could best develop and control the nascent powers wherewith her Risorgimento had endowed her. His was not, indeed, the mental *Allgemeinheit*, which knows how to interpret man and nature in verse that appeals to all nations and all ages. But in his poetry the third Italy saw herself reflected in her purest and serenest aspect, and her ideals linked on to many, if not all, the most cherished traditions of her past.

THE HYMN TO SATAN

To Satan

THOU first cause, whence all things
Their being inherit,
Who art Reason and Sense,
Who art Matter and Spirit:

While a sparkle and perfume
In wine-cups arise,
Like the soul of a man
Flashing forth from his eyes,

While earth smiles below
And the sun shines above,
While soft voices murmur
The first words of love,

While hills hymn the secret
Glad nuptials of earth,
While the rich plain is throbbing
In pangs of new birth,

For thee my bold fancy
From bonds is released,
I invoke thee, O Satan,
Our lord of the feast.

Priest, chanting and sprinkling
No succour shall find thee,
For never shall Satan
Get him behind thee.

See, red rust doth darken
The mystical blade
Of the Archangel Michael;
Unwinged and dismayed

He is hurled in the void
Heaven's battlements over.
The thunder lies frozen
In the hand of Jehovah.

Like meteors and planets
Whose light is all spent,
The angels rain down
From the domed firmament.

In all Matter existent
For ever awake,
King of all that eye sees,
King of all that hands make,

Alone lives great Satan.
He holds his Empire
In the dark eye, where flickers
A tremulous fire,

Which now smoulders low,
And all wooers resists,
Now tearfully flashes,
Entices, insists.

With gladness he gleams
In the juice of the grape,
Holds fast fickle joy
When it longs to escape,

He e'en restores life
On the eve to depart,
Puts sorrow at bay,
And sows love in the heart.

Thou makest, O Satan,
My verse thine abode
An thou burst from my bosom
To challenge the God,

Whom base Popes adore
And Kings cruel as they,
If like thunder thou smitest
Their souls with dismay.

For thee Agramainio,
Astartë, Adon
Lived in poem and picture
And breathed from the stone.

When Ionian zephyrs
Blew soft o'er the sea
'Neath the blessing of Venus
Anadyomene.

For thee on Mount Lebanon's
High cedar grove
Fair Cypris established
Tribunals of love:

For thee was the frenzy
Of dance and of choir,
For thee were chaste virgins
Enflamed with love's fire,

Where the palm-woods of Edom
Make fragrant the breeze,
Where Cyprus gleams white
In the foam of her seas.

What avails him the wrath
Of the fierce Nazarene,
Tho' with barbarous rites
Of his love-feast obscene,

With the torch of the priest,
He demolished thy shrine
And cast on the earth
All that Greece held divine?

Tho' exiled, of helpers
Thou feltest no dearth,
For the people enthroned thee
As God of the hearth.

Then the breast of a woman
Thou mad'st thine abode;
It throbbed with thy presence,
Her lover and God;

The sorceress pallid
With unending woe
Thou bad'st to the succour
Of weak nature go.

By thee was the alchemist's
Dull eye unsealed,
Through thee the magician
At length saw revealed

Beyond the dim cloister's
Enclosure a new
World of beauty, undreamed of,
Bright heavens of blue.

To escape thee, whose power
Thro' all things is spread,
The hermit forlorn
To the Thebaid fled.

O soul, that forsak'st all
Thou lovest most well,
Of the mercies of Satan
Let Heloise tell.

Self-starved, in sackcloth
Thou groanest in vain:
'Mid the dirge of the Psalmist
He mingles the strain

Of the Virgil and Horace
Thou sought'st to forget:
'Mid the black nuns beside thee
Strange forms doth he set,

Greek women; than rose-coloured
Morning e'en fairer,
He bringeth Lycoris,
He bringeth Glicera.

In the cell, too, thy sleepless
Eyes often behold
More phantoms he sends thee
From brave days of old.

From the pages of Livy
He wakes to new life
Bold tribunes and consuls,
The forum's fierce strife.

And his spirit impels thee,
O Monk, with strange pride
In thy country, to mount up
The Capitol's side.

And ye whom the fierce flames
Knew not to consume,
Huss and Wicliffe, your voices,
With accent of doom,

Are borne down the breeze
As ye watch night and day:
"A new age is dawning,
The old fades away."

Now mitre and crown dread
The hot thunderbolt:
From the cloister there mutters
The sound of Revolt:

With voice as of tempest
No yoke may confine
Cries Savonarola,
Our great Florentine.

And Luther his cassock
Casts off in disdain;
O Man, let thy mind too
Cast off its old chain!

Shine now in bright splendour
With flame girded on!
Blaze, World, in white glory!
Great Satan hath won.

A monster, a terror
On earth is set free,
It runs o'er the forest,
It runs o'er the sea.

Volcano-like towering
With smoke and with fire,
More vast than the plains,
Than the high mountains higher;

It soars o'er abysses
And downward cloth sweep
To hide in black caverns
And plunge in the deep.

It bursts forth unfettered:
From shore unto shore
With noise as of whirlwind
In tyrannous roar,

With breath as of whirlwind
Is thundered the cry:
"Ye peoples, great Satan
In might passeth by,

"In benison passeth
From land unto land
On his chariot of fire
No man may withstand."

All hail then, O Satan,
Revolt too! All hail!
And Reason predestined
O'er all to prevail.

Lo, here on thine altar
Our offerings are spread!
The priest thou hast conquered,
Jehovah is dead.

HYMN TO SATAN

(trans. by Emily A. Tribe)

To thee of all being
The first cause immense
Of matter and spirit,
Of reason and sense.

Whilst in the full goblet
Shall sparkle the wine,
So bright through the pupil
The souls of men shine,

Whilst earth still is smiling,
And the sun smiles above,
And men are exchanging
Their sweet words of love,

Thrills mystic of Hymen
Through high mountains course,
And broad plains are heaving
With life's fertile force,

On thee in verse daring,
From tight rein released,
On thee I call, Satan,
The king of the feast.

Away aspersorium,
With priest who would bind!
Priest, not at thy bidding
Gets Satan behind.

Behold, rust is eating
The edge of the blade
In the hand of great Michael
The faithful displayed.

The displumed Archangel
Descends to the void,
The thunderbolt's frozen
Jehovah employed.

Faint pallid meteors,
Wan stars void of light,
Like rain down from heaven
Fall angels in flight.

In matter aye sleepless
Of forces the spring,
King of phenomena,
Of forms lord and king.

Here only lives Satan,
His power supreme
In a dark eye flashes
With tremulous gleam,

Whether it languidly
Retreats and rebels,
Or bright and audacious
Provokes and compels.

In gay blood it sparkles
That's pressed from the vine,
Whose gift of swift pleasure
Shall never decline,

Which can to our fleeting
Life new strength impart,
Which puts off our sorrows,
To love gives a heart.

'Tis thou that inspirest
The song that doth rise
In my bosom, O Satan,
When that god it defies,

On whom guilty pontiffs
And cruel kings call;
Men's minds thou so shakest
As when lightnings fall.

Ahriman and Adonis,
Astarte, to thee,
Canvas, marble and paper
All lived and were free.

When Venus new risen
From billowing seas
Serenely made happy
Ionia's breeze.

On Lebanon quivered
The trees at thy name,
When to gentle Cypria
Her risen love came.

Thee chorus and dances
In joy celebrate,
Love pure and virginal
To thee dedicate

Mid the palm-trees fragrant
Of Araby's land,
Where whitens the sea-foam
On Cyprian strand.

What matter if fury
Of fierce Nazarene
From ritual barbaric
Of love-feast obscene

Hath set with blest torches
The temples on fire,
And Argolis' idols
Hath hurled in the mire.

In cottages lowly
A refuge dost find,
Amid household Lares
Folk keep thee in mind.

The God and the lover
A woman's warm breast
With his ardent spirit
Once having possessed,

Thou turnest the witch
Whom long searching makes pale
To lend succour to nature,
O'er disease to prevail.

Thou to the motionless
Eye of the alchemist,
In sight of the magus
Who dares to resist,

Beyond the dull cloister
Its gates set ajar,
Revealest in brightness
New heavens afar.

In lonely Thebaid
The wretched monks hide
From thee and things worldly
In safety to bide.

Ah, doubtful soul standing
Where life's roads divide,
See, Satan is kindly,
Heloise at thy side!

In vain with rough sackcloth
Thy flesh dost maltreat,
From Maro and Flaccus
He verse will repeat

Betwixt psalms of David;
Twixt weeping and dirge
He causes beside thee
Delphic forms to emerge.

Amongst those companions
Though garbed in black weeds
With rosy Lycoris
Glycera he leads.

But other the phantoms
When finer the age,
At times he awakens
From Livy's full page,

When tribunes and consuls
And vast crowds that thrill
With ardour and passion
That sleepless cell fill,

He to the Capitol
Thy land to set free
Of Italic pride dreaming,
O monk, urges thee.

And you, Huss and Wycliffe,
No fury of flames
Could stifle your voices'
Prophetic acclaims.

Send forth on the breezes
Your watch-cry sublime
"A new age is dawning,
Fulfilled is the time!"

Already are trembling
Both mitre and crown,
And cloistered seclusion
Rebellion breaks down.

Then fighting and preaching
Under the stola
Comes Fra Girolamo;
Savonarola.

The cowl Luther cast off.
And freedom he brought:
So cast off thy fetters,
Be free, human thought!

And shine forth resplendent,
Encircled with flames,
Arise Matter, Satan
The victory claims.

A beautiful monster,
A terrible birth,
Runs over the ocean,
Runs over the earth.

Volcano like flashes
Through dim smoke it lowers,
It scales lofty mountains,
Broad plains it devours.

It spans the abysses,
In caverns it hides
And through the deep cleft ways
Invisible glides;

Then comes forth undaunted,
From coast to coast hies,
As from some fierce whirlwind
It sends forth its cries.

As breath of the whirlwind
Spreads out on the vast
Expanse, O ye nations,
Great Satan goes past.

From place to place passes
Beneficent he
On his chariot of fire
Untrammelled and free.

All hail to thee, Satan!
Rebellion, all hail!
Hail, power of reason,
Avenge and prevail!

To thee arise incense
And holy vows paid,
Thou, Satan, hast vanquished
The god by priests made.

A Satana

ATE, de l' essere
Principio immenso,
Materia e spirito,
Ragione e senso;

Mentre ne' calici
Il vin scintilla
Si come l' anima
Ne la pupilla;

Mentre sorridono
La terra e il sole
E si ricambiano
D' amor parole,

E cone un fremito
D'imene arcano
Da' monti e palpita
Fecondo it piano;

A to disfrenasi
Il verso ardito,
Te invoco, o Satana,
Re del convito.

Via l' aspersorio
Prete, e it tuo metro!
No, prete, Satana
Non torna in dietro!

Vedi: la ruggine
Rode a Michele
Il brando mistico,
Ed it fedele

Spennato arcangelo
Cade nel vano.
Ghiacciato è il fulmine
A Geova in mano.

Meteore pallide,
Pianeti spenti,
Piovono gli angeli
Da i firmamenti.

Ne la materia
Che mai non dorme,
Re de i fenomeni,
Re de le forme,

Sol vive Satana.
Ei tien impero
Nel lampo tremulo
D' un occhio nero,

O ver the languido
Sfugga e resista,
Od acre ed umido
Pròvochi, insista.

Brilla de' grappoli
Nel lieto sangue,
Per cui la rapida
Gioia non langue,

Che la fuggevole
Vita ristora,
Che it dolor proroga,
Che amor ne incora.

Tu spirt, o Satana,
Nel verso mio,
Se dal sen rompemi
Sfidando il dio

De' rei pontefici,
De' re crüenti;
E come fulmine
Scuoti le menti.

A te, Agramainio,
Adone, Astarte,
E marmi vissero
E tele e carte,

Quando le ioniche
Aure serene
Beò la Venere
Anadiomene.

A te del Libano
Fremean le piante,
De l' alma Cipride
Risorto amante:

A te ferveano
Le danze e i cori,
A te i virginei
Candidi amori,

Tra le odorifere
Palme d' Idume,
Dove biancheggiano
Le ciprie spume.

Che val se barbaro
Il nazareno
Furor de l' agapi
Dal rito osceno

Con sacra fiaccola
I templi t' arse
E i segni argolici
A terra sparse?

Te accolse profugo
Tra gli dèi lari
La plebe memore
Ne i casolari.

Quindi un femineo
Sen palpitante
Empiendo, fervido
Nume ed amante,

La strega pallida
D' eterna cura
Volgi a soccorrere
L' egra natura.

Tu a l' occhio immobile
De l' alchimista,
Tu de l' indocile
Mago a la vista,

Del chiostro torpido
Oltre i cancelli,
Riveli i fulgidi
Cieli novelli.

A la Tebaide
Te ne le cose
Fuggendo, it monaco
Triste s'ascose.

O dal tuo tramite
Alma divisa,
Benigno è Satana;
Ecco Eloisa.

In van ti maceri
Ne l' aspro sacco:
Il verso ei mormora
Di Maro e Flacco

Tra la davidica
Nenia ed it pianto;
E, forme delfiche,
A to da canto,

Rosee ne orrida
Compagnia nera;
Mena Licoride,
Mena Glicera.

Ma d' altre imagini
D' età piú bella
Talor si popola
L' insonne cella.

Ei, da le pagine
Di Livio, ardenti
Tribuni, consoli,
Turbe frementi

Sveglia; e fantastico
D' italo orgoglio
Te spinge, o monaco,
Su 'l Campidoglio.

E voi, the it rabido
Rogo non strusse,
Voci fatidiche,
Wicleff ed Husse,

A l' aura it vigile
Grido mandate:
S' innova it secolo
Piena è l' etate.

E già già tremano
Mitre e corone:
Dal chiostro brontola
La ribellione,

E pugna e prèdica
Sotto la stola
Di fra' Girolamo
Savonarola.

Gittò la tonaca
Martin Lutero:
Gitta i tuoi vincoli,
Uman pensiero,

E splendi e folgora
Di fiamme cinto;
Materia, inalzati:
Satana ha vinto.

Un bello e orribile
Mostro si sferra,
Cone gli oceani
Cone la terra:

Corusco e fumido
Come i vulcani,
I monti supera,
Divora i piani;

Sorvola i baratri,
Poi si nasconde
Per antri incogniti,
Per vie profonde;

Ed esce; e indomito
Di lido in lido
Come di turbine
Manda il suo grido,

Come di turbine
L' alito spande:
Ei passa, o popoli,
Satana it grande.

Passa benefico
Di loco in loco
Su l' infrenabile
Carro del foco.

Salute, o Satana,
O ribellione,
O forza vindice
De la ragione!

Sacri a to salgano
Gl' incensi e i vóti!
Hai vinto it Geova
De i sacerdoti.

from
EVIA GRAVIA

For The Marriage Of A Geologist
(Prof. G. C.)

EXPLORER of the underworld, from whom
Shy Nature, shrinking, hides in vain distress,
For to thy love in her deep bridal room
She must unveil her virgin loveliness,

Lift up thine eyes! This once forsake thy gloom
And breathe the air that living men doth bless!
Here smiles on thee a maiden in the bloom
Of youth, decked by her mother in bridal dress.

Here shalt thou learn if Love prove stronger, when
He shows where Etna's secret fires reside,
Or sweeter in a woman's heart may reign.

So with fresh courage—for she will not chide—
From her soft bosom turning shalt thou then
In holy Nature seek thy other bride.

from
GIAMBI ED EPODI

Meminisse Horret

MAKE fast every door, from all exit withhold me,
And wrap ye the thickest of veils round my head!
The shades of a horrible nightmare enfold me:
With yellow I 've witnessed the skies overspread.

A foul stench of sewers and corpses was stealing
From the ancient Palazzo which faces us there:
"To the gallows with Piero Capponi" were pealing
The Bargello's bells over city and square.

And from the fair hills, which, when danger impended,
Roared death to the German invader, a loud
Sound of litanies slowly came down to me blended
With the *Misereres* of a fear-stricken crowd.

Ferruccio with hands humbly clasped lay prostrated
And begged of the wretch Maramaldo his life:
And Gian della Bella, his hood raised, related
How Berto had threatened his nose with the knife.

And Dante tricked out as a clown I saw playing
Within Santa Croce the role of a guide:
"Oh, sirs, don't be nervous of us," he kept saying;
"Come in, sirs: our patrons are ye, and our pride.

"What matter if shame more or less pay our gentry?
I'm a poet: of haggling I don't know the trick.
To the Ghetto of Italy all men have entry,
The people of Italy who'd deign to kick?"

By a tombstone crouched Machiavel: to another
Who passed him he slyly winked, whispering low
(For I heard him): "A breast fair and broad has my mother
And soft, flowing tresses: she never says no.

"To the forums her paramours flock without payment,
Their Dorian halls are the scene of her lust:
On the Capitol's height she ungirdles her raiment,
And yields herself naked, o'er Scipio's dust."

FOR GIUSEPPE MONTI AND GAETANO TOGNETTI
MARTYRS OF ITALIAN JUSTICE

I

STRUGGLING through fog and gloom the dreary light
Of day dawns over Rome:
Life faintly stirs: but silence dread as night
Still broods o'er hearth and home.

Upon the gardens of the Vatican
Weighs like a pall of lead
November: no birds sing, the sky is wan
And pale, the trees are dead.

Yellow and white and grey the drifting leaves
Drop softly to the ground—
A mournful shower, that ever deeper weaves
A winding-sheet around

The statues, youthful gods of Grecian art
Who, in the times gone by,
Have watched the glories of the world depart
And now seem fain to die.

That day the High Priest woke in cheerful mood:
Naught but grey skies to see,
Framed in the gilded casement, was right good:
He rubbed his hands with glee.

Though the fair face of Nature seemed deformed
In horror of coming death,
Feeling his limbs still by the soft sheets warmed,
"Yea, I am strong," he saith.

"My Sainted Predecessor, many a year
Since thy brave deed hath fled.
Thou, Peter, wert contented with an ear,
I shall cut off the head.

"This time upon *our* side the legions gather,
  Of Jesus take no reck!
For He, shut up in Sacro Cuore, by Father
  Curci is held in check.

"I am a strong old man: to heart and head
  I feel fresh life-blood given:
Put a new edge upon the axe which sped
  Locatelli to heaven.

"Let it be brandished flashing bright and bold,
  Subtle like thought and swift:
Erect a goodly gibbet spend the gold
  Of Menabrea's gift.

"Frenchmen, put by Voltaire's *Mahomet*; in short,
  Come show a just repentance,
And, as my assessors in the Sacred Court,
  Help ratify our sentence.

"In San Niccola grant indulgences!
  Expose the Body of God,
And before Italy my daughter these
  Two heads that drip with blood!"

II

And yet thy hair is white: yet flow the fountains
Of life more sluggish in thee day by day,
Dwindling in heart and brain as in the mountains
A cloud is lost and slowly melts away.

O grant them now their lives! To one his twenty
Years are proud heralds of nobler years in store,
And in his breast spring youthful hopes in plenty
E'en though he languish on thy dungeon floor.

The other sees three children grow about him
Like chestnut shoots beneath the parent tree:
But now they droop, and their sad mother without him
At sunset trembles, when she thinks of thee.

Ah, long ago, when by the Jordan river,
By cities glad with olive, the gentle soul
Of Christ, the young Prince, mighty to deliver,
Drew all men unto Him to make them whole,

No mothers trembled: nay, from death He frees us:
For did not Nain see Him death's power destroy?
And whether more to kiss her son or Jesus
The weeping widow knew not in her joy.

The little blue-eyed children sought His blessing
Lovely He was and meek—they trusted Him.
And, while He stood their golden curls caressing
With sinless hands, His eyes with tears were dim.

But thou, in whose vile soul no love of God is,
Smitest with crime-stained fist these heads to earth,
In blood, that streams from their dead fathers' bodies,
Stiffing the tender blossoms at their birth.

Thou in the sight of parents in their anguish
(Whose limbs like thine are old and tottering)
Diggest graves for their sons, while yet they languish
In prison, O bloody cleric, unwarlike king.

Priest, prove them false who say that thou dost glory
None e'er from thy black den safe issueth.
Come, Christian Polyphemus, deny the story
That thou in thirty days canst nurture death.

Oh, clasp him to thy bosom, crying: "Heaven
Bids peace and blessing flow from the Papal Throne,"
And thou shalt feel new life-blood to thee given
By that young heart that beats against thine own. . . .

Fixed in his cruel purpose he remaineth
(Our prayers are vain, he scoffs at our distress):
Mercy and love as weakness he disdaineth,
In him alone old age was pitiless.

III

'Tis better so! Blood of the slain rise up
To heaven! Hasten fate!
Be as red wine of vengeance in the cup
Our sons to inebriate—

Our sons, whom we had taught to love, to whom
The Future now appears
So bright, let Hate thus early with its gloom
O'ercast their boyhood's years!

Look, listen, opposed continents, ye mountains
Rebellious 'gainst the sky,
Isles of the ocean fair with woods and fountains,
And ships that travel by;

And thou, O Europe, wayworn Handmaid, who
Dost fall and rise again;
And thou, who 'cross the Atlantic dost pursue
The star of William Penn;

And ye, whom shafts of tropic sunlight pierce,
Who snakes and tyrants feed,
Vast Africa and Asia, and ye fierce,
Ye coloured tribes, give heed!

And thou, O Sun divine, see this old man's
Bland, honest features, see
His bloodstained hands and healthy countenance!
The Chouans' angel he!

He, ere the executioner hath washed
The fatal scaffold, drives out
To gloat on people's horror, unabashed
Their righteous grief to flout.

He, struck with ghastly madness, wags his head
Like a drunk man, and feels
A bestial desire to see the red
Drops splash his gilded wheels.

Old man, the cruel pageants, that with glee
Thou plannest, we disdain.
He who the two La Galas saved bids thee
Cut off men's heads in vain.

Two thou hast quenched: but thousands wait the call,
Yea, and more thousands still.
Our white tents gleam by every city wall,
They gleam on plain and hill,

Where'er spring love and light, in every region
That noble hearts can cherish:
Old man, we are the sacred Theban legion,
And we can never perish.

Our way is strewn with graves, but like an altar
Each grave is decked with flowers:
The memory of the dead burns: shall we falter
In this great work of ours?

Nay, see us all join hands, the sage, the bard,
Warrior and artisan:
Easy is now that which was once so hard—
We threatened the Vatican.

Fed by the martyr's blood, bright torches quiver
Fanned by the breeze awhile,
Until at length, above the ancient river,
Shall fall th' accursed pile.

Thereafter Tiber's dark-haired nymph shall rove
'Mid moss-grown stones, and tell
The pilgrim how these are the ruins of
A shame unspeakable.'

Giuseppe Mazzini

A MARBLE giant, high o'er the sea that cowers
'Neath her bare cliffs, stands Genoa proud and fair:
Even thus, unmoved by days of dark despair,
Grand o'er the restless century he towers.

From cliffs, whence young Columbus used to stare
Across the waves to a new land, with powers
Of vision as keen, he saw a time that dowers
With Freedom the third Italy:—he, the heir

Of Gracchus' lion-heart and Dante's mind,
His eyes fixed on that goal, moved onward through
A graveyard, with a nation dead behind.

Exiled for long, long years, his face, that knew
No smile, he lifts to Heaven severe yet kind,
Musing: "Thou only, O Ideal, art true."

On The Fifth Anniversary of the Battle of Mentana

EACH year, when thy anniversary,
Mentana, like a sighing
Voice o'er the hills, goes mournfully
Reproaching our neglect,
  O'er hill and plain in companies
The noble dead come flying,
And at Nomentum haughtily
Stand on the mounds erect.

They are spirits tall and beautiful,
Not skeletons unsightly;
The rosy mists of evening
Veil them as they float by:
  Thro' their red wounds shine radiantly
The virgin stars, and lightly
With their long locks are mingled
The clouds that sweep the sky.

"Now that on beds unvisited
By sleep are mothers mourning,
Now that young brides are dreaming of
Love that was ours in vain,
  We that were wounded, slain for thee,
From Tartarus are returning,
To greet thee, O our Italy,
To see thee once again.

"As a knight would cast his mantle on
A muddy path, defiling
The gay green silk right gallantly
That his lady thereon might tread,
  For thee we cast down fearlessly
Our lives, at black Fate smiling;
Yet thou can'st live forgetful of
Those who for thee lie dead.

"To other men, sweet Italy,
Thy smiles and gifts are given;
But the dead of what was dear to them
In life are forgetful ne'er.
  Yet Rome is ours: as champions
Of her great name we have striven;
Let us fly on to the Capitol,
Let us fly to triumph there."

On like dark clouds those companies
Of dead o'er heaven go streaming:
A nameless awe on Italian
Breasts, as they pass, doth fall:
  Hushed are the gilded galleries
Where music and lights are gleaming:
Men hear the thunder muttering
On the lofty Quirinal.

Meanwhile below to the city of
Gracchus ever more thickly
Troop in, sleek-bellied and infamous,
The "Chevaliers d'industrie";
  They say: "If skies be thundery,
Let 's fill our pockets quickly;
Then come the flood, we welcome it:
For what will be, will be."

THE SONG OF LOVE

FAIR in her fair days rose Rocca Paolina:
With cannon did her buttressed ramparts bristle!
Pope Paul the third planned her one morn between a
Text of Bembo and his Latin Missal.

"Too freely do my sheep who pasture under
Perugia's precipices stray from me:
For chastening, God the Father hath the thunder,
And I, His vicar, will use artillery.

"*Coelo tonantem* Horace sings, and louder
Than the stormwind God speaketh in His rage:
'Return, my sheep,' I'll cry with shot and powder,
'To Sharon's and Engaddi's pasturage.'

"Yet hearken, since the Augustan age, Sangallo,
With us renews its glories, consummate,
Worthy of Rome and thee, a work to hallow
The golden years of our Pontificate."

He spoke, and to defend her maiden honour
Sangallo arched her round on every side,
And cast a veil of snow-white marble on her
And girdled her with towers for her pride.

In Latin distichs she was celebrated
By Molza: and the Paraclete rained down
In bombs and from the mortars unabated
His more than sevenfold gifts upon the town.

And yet the people are a dog, which biteth
The stones it cannot hurl, as well ye know,
And specially on fortresses delighteth
To exercise its iron fangs, and so

To shatter them, then lies with joyous barking
Stretched on the ruined walls, till up it springs
And rushes off, some novel quarry marking,
To other stones and other cudgellings.

So in Perugia it befell. Where dim in
The shade of that stern pile the city lay,
Love laugheth now, and merrily the women
And children prattle in the sun of May.

And through the spacious azure ever higher
The bright sun mounts, till far Abruzzi's snows
Glisten, and yet with more intense desire
Of Love on Umbrian hill and pasture glows.

Where in the rosy light serenely rising
The mountains interweave their perfect lines,
Until each tender contour melts and dies in
The golden violet haze that o'er them shines.

Is 't, Italy, thy fragrant hair strewn over
Thy nuptial bed, 'twixt seas to east and west,
Which 'neath the kisses of th' eternal lover
Trembles in scattered ringlets to thy breast?

What'er it be, I feel Spring with me blending,
And all my thoughts a sapphire radiance stains;
I feel the sighs, ascending and descending
"Twixt earth and heaven, throb through all my veins.

Each novel sight mine eager eye descrieth
Awakes some old affection in my heart;
"Love, Love!" my tongue to earth and heaven crieth
In words that from my lips unbidden start.

Do I embrace the heavens, or doth the ocean
Of Being absorb me in its timeless calm? . . .
Ah, this poor verse expressing my emotion
Is but one note of the Eternal Psalm.

From Umbrian villages, which love to bury
Themselves in dark rifts of the Apennine;
From Tyrrhene castles standing solitary
Above the green hills rich in corn and wine;

From plains, whence 'mid the ploughed-up bones and armour
Dread Rome still threatens in defeat's black day;
From German forts, which watched the ancient farmer,
Like nesting falcons brooding o'er their prey;

From gloomy-towered palaces the nation
Built that she might her foreign lords defy;
From churches which, as if in supplication,
Stretch forth long marble arms unto the sky;

From happy suburbs up the hillside creeping
Towards the city, old and dark and hoar,
Like villeins hasting homeward after reaping
To share the grain that fills the threshing-floor;

From convents, nestled in the valleys, ringing
Their bells o'er suburb and o'er city-street,
Like cuckoos in the leafless branches singing
Two notes, where joy and pain so strangely meet;

From roads and from piazzas rich in story,
Where, e'en as one blithe morn of May attires
The oaks and rose-trees in their summer glory,
Burst into bloom the Free Art of our sires;

O'er fields where now the tender green blades quiver,
O'er vineyards clinging to the steep hillside,
O'er lakes and many a far-off shining river,
O'er woods and snow-clad summits far and wide;

From sunny cots, o'er which the blue smoke lingers,
'Mid all the noisy mills and thundering weirs,
Leaps up one song sung by a thousand singers,
One hymn wherein are blent a thousand prayers:

"Greeting, ye human races bowed with sorrow
All passes, naught can die: too much we dare
To hate and suffer. Learn to love! The morrow
Shall thus be holier and the world more fair."

What is that radiance, like some new Aurora's
Greeting the sun, on yonder mountain height?
Do then Madonnas as of old pass o'er us,
Treading these hills on paths of rosy light?

Madonnas Perugino saw descending,
Thro' pearly April sunsets pure and mild,
With outstretched arms, in adoration bending
Divinely meek before the Holy Child?

Nay, 'tis a new Madonna whom we call on,
Justice and Love, the Ideal for which we strive!
Blessed be those who for her sake have fallen,
Blessed be those who for her sake shall live!

For Priests and Tyrants naught care I!
Unsteady, Infirm, and old as their old Gods are they.
I cursed the Pope ten years ago, I'm ready
To reconcile myself with him to-day.

The poor old man! Who knows if he is yearning
In vain for love? E'en now his thoughts may be
To his own Sinigaglia fondly turning
Where it lies mirrored in the Adrian sea.

Open the Vatican! I would embrace thee,
Who ne'er from out thy self-made prison wilt pass.
Come, Citizen Mastai, 'twill not disgrace thee;
The toast is "Freedom," drain with me one glass!

from
INTERMEZZO

INTERLUDE

9

NOT against thee shall my Muse vent her spleen,
    O Land, to which my love
Ne'er paid its debt, which I have only seen
    Through tearful dreams, where move

Ghosts of my childhood. Oh, on the mountain-side
    By the Etruscan sea,
Farewell, Versilia mine, Ligurian pride
    Of Counts of Lombardy!

If from thy women my Tuscan accent got
    Its strength with sweetness blent,
Thy marbles, Serravezza, I ask not
    To build my monument.

Lest in the past my name forgotten sink,
    Far from my cradle I 've sought
For other marbles, while I write and think—
    Marbles which cost me naught.

Other the glories. O like diamond white
    Amid the Ægean blue,
Paros, from whose Marpesian side the bright
    Pure Gods of Hellas grew,

Thou, who 'twixt Naxos, where Ariadne slept
    Upon a breast divine,
And wandering Delos, whence Apollo leapt,
    The Grecian's god and mine,

Sawest Archilochus uncurb his pent
    Iambics 'neath thy skies,
And heardest, 'mid the halcyon's lament,
    Evenus' elegies,

To me th' Archilochus of Italy
    Who play Evenus' part,
But better, give so much stone as may be
    Tomb for my weary heart.

This heart, which ne'er asked love, but only cares
    After ideals to strain,
And which, hard stricken in the fray, prepares
    To die: lo, I would fain

Now bury it: sweet may the labour be
    Which to that work belongs!
O Paros, Greece, ancient serene, give me
    Thy marbles and thy songs.

from
RIME NUOVE

To Rhyme

HAIL thee, Rhyme, to bonds committed
By quick-witted
Troubadours with careful art:
But thou sprightly, rushest lightly,
Gushest brightly
Sparkling from the people's heart.

Oh, 'twixt kiss and kiss how gladly,
Where most madly
Whirl the dancers, lips let fly
Thee, who in two turns at latest
Deftly matest
Hope with Memory, sigh with sigh!

Oh, how gaily wert thou floated
By full-throated
Voices after hours of toil,
As the triple reaper-chorus
With sonorous
Triple note stamped on the soil!

Dreadful down the breeze, when shouted
O'er the routed,
Roared thy voice on stricken fields,
While the blood-stained javelins rattle
Hurled in battle
'Gainst the serried iron shields.

Roland's sword thou heardest shatter
Rocks and batter
Roncival: come night, come morn,
Highland echoes unto lowland
"Roland, Roland"
When thou windest his great horn.

Then of black Bavieca singing
Rod'st thou, clinging
To his rough mane, gallant, free;
Where the Cid's gay pennon glances,
All Romance is
Mounted on his horse with thee.

Then in Rhone's swift torrent plunging,
There expunging
From thy hair its dust-stained hues,
Thou, sweet nightingales outvying,
Flittest sighing
Through the orchards of Toulouse.

Thou Love's pilot wast in feudal
Times, when Rudel
Sailed forth in his ship of ships:
Bearer of the burning kisses,
Which he presses,
Dying, on his lady's lips.

Turn, return grave Dante calls thee
And installs thee
By his side: with thee he trod
Other paths through realms infernal,
Clomb th' eternal
Mountain and thence soared to God.

Empress, who o'er metre bearest
Rule, O fairest
Queen of Latin poetry,
Lo, a rebel, long disloyal,
Craves thy royal
Grace and pays thee homage free.

Rhyme, among our sires renowned,
Courted, crowned,
Thee I too will venerate.
Fare thee well: with flowers salute my
Friends, but shoot thy
Arrows against those I hate.

THE SONNET

DANTE gave it the Cherubim's swift wing,
Pouring around it azure air and gold:
To Petrarch 'twas a channel divine to hold
The tears that through his verse run murmuring:

Tasso for it bade Tibur's Muses bring
The honey and ambrosia that of old
Horace and Virgil ate: Alfieri rolled
It thunderlike 'gainst slave and cruel king:

Ugo breathed into it the nightingales'
Music beneath Ionian cypresses,
And girt it with his own acanthus blooms.

Sixth am I not, but last—those ecstasies,
Tears, perfumes, passion, art, like twice-told tales
I, solitary, sing unto the tombs.

CONVERSATION WITH TREES

THEE, who untrodden cliff and mournful plain
Shadest, thought-wrinkled Oak, I love not now,
Since thou hast decked the forehead of insane
Destroyers of cities with thy gracious bough.

Nor do I yearn for thee, proud Laurel, for thou
Art false and insolent: whether thy vain
Green leaves mock dismal winter or the brow
Of Rome's bald Cæsars, thee do I disdain.

I love thee, Vine, who 'mid thy brown stones seen
Dost laugh in leafy splendour, and the cup
Prepare of wise forgetfulness of life:

Yet dearer still the Pine: may he between
Four boards—a polished coffin—at last shut up
All my heart's dark despair and fruitless strife.

THE OX

I LOVE thee, holy ox: a soothing sense
Of power and peace thou lodgest in my heart.
How solemn, like a monument, thou art,
Watching the pastures fertile and immense!

Or 'neath the yoke with calmness how intense
Dost thou to man's quick toil thine aid impart!
He shouts and goads thee: patient of the smart,
Thine eyes, slow turning, claim more reverence.

From thy broad nostrils, black and moist, doth rise
Thy breath in fragrant incense: like a psalm
Swells on the air thy lowing's joyful strain.

Austerely sweet are thy grave emerald eyes,
And in their depths is mirrored, wide and calm,
All the divine green silence of the plain.

Virgil

AS when the gracious moon climbs up the sky,
Drenching parched fields with dew on summer eves,
The murmuring brook, 'twixt low banks rippling by,
Of her white beams a silvery network weaves;

The secret nightingale among the leaves
Fills the vast calm with throbbing melody,
So sweet th' entranced wayfarer half believes
Time is not, and his fair-haired love seems nigh;

And the bereaved mother who wept in vain
Beside a grave is soothed and comforted,
When the grey dawn doth over heaven shine:

Mountains and distant sea smile out again,
A fresh breeze stirs the branches overhead:
Such is thy verse to me, O poet divine.

"Funere Mersit Acerbo"

O THOU that sleepest 'neath th' enamelled sward
Of that low Tuscan hill, and by thee lies
Our father, in thy tomb hast thou not heard
Amid the grass a voice that softly cries?

It is my baby boy, who hastens toward
Thy dreary gate and knocks—he with whom dies
Thy sacred name: the life thou foundest hard,
O'er-hard to bear, he too thus early flies.

Ah, no! For till the shadow thrust him dead
To your cold, cheerless shores, he knew no other
Care but to play 'mid flowers, where bright dreams shed

Their radiance o'er him. Oh, receive him, brother,
In thy dark mansions, for he turns his head
To the sweet sunlight, sobbing for his mother.

St. Mary of the Angels

HOW spacious, brother Francis, and how high
Is this fair dome of il Vignola spread
Above the spot where thou in agony
Layed'st naked with crossed arms, the earth thy bed!

'Tis hot July: and o'er the plain, long wed
To labour, floats the love-song. Would that I
Caught in the Umbrian song thy accent sped,
Thy face reflected in the Umbrian sky!

And where the mountain-village stands outlined
'Gainst heav'n, a mild, lone radiance o'er thee poured,
As from thy Paradise that openeth,

Would I could see thee—arms outstretched and mind
Intent on God—singing: "Praised be the Lord!
For death of the body, our dear sister Death."

DANTE

DANTE, how comes it that my vows I pay
To thy stern image? that the sun hath seen
Me poring o'er the verse "that made thee lean"
Both setting and when he brings back the day?

For me no prayer doth sainted Lucy say,
No aid fair Mathilde lends to lave me clean,
For me have Beatrice and her lover been
Voyagers in vain upon their starry way.

I hate thy holy Empire: and my sword
In Val d' Olona would have cloven the head
Of thy good Frederick with his crown thereon.

Empire and Church lie ruined and abhorred,
While heavenward soars thy song unconquered:
The poet endures, tho' Jove be dead and gone.

"Away With Your Advice"

"CHARMING our ladies, our young men adorn
Themselves right bravely: poet, come and spread
Thy chorus of winged stanzas overhead.
Strew flowers thyself. No need our loves to scorn.

"Why is thy verse so raw? Why sow a thorn
Within our hearts? Forget. The Fates have led
Thee to th' Enchanted Garden, smiles are shed
On thee by Beauty. Is earth then so forlorn?"—

Now to indignant Juvenal go say:
"Be not so frantic! Smile. Take our advice,
Change to Glyconics thy fierce Hexameters";

And, when great Dante hurls his burning verse
Up out of Hell, down out of Paradise,
Just soothe their fury in your *café au lait*.

Sunlight and Love

FLEECY and white the clouds are westward streaming;
On mart and street, as the dank mist retires,
Smiles out the sky: the sun's triumphant fires
Greet the vast world with human labour teeming.

All rose-red stands the great cathedral, seeming
To shout hosannas with its thousand spires
And saints of gold: while the brown-feathered choirs
Of wheeling falcons swoop around it screaming.

E'en so, when love's sweet smile hath set me free
From the dark clouds that weighed on me so long,
My soul expands and suns itself: I see

Life's great ideal with its radiant throng
Of blessings smile at me: a harmony
Is every thought, and every sense a song.

"HERE REIGNETH LOVE"

WHERE art thou? And for whom, O lady mine,
Dost temper the keen ray of thy dark eyes?
For whom dost thou in soft tones harmonise
The secret music of that heart of thine?

Dost thou, my sweet, 'mid flowers and grass recline,
Dreamily gazing at the windy skies?
Or of some wooing stream art thou the prize,
To whose embrace thou dost thy limbs resign?

Oh, whereso'er thou art, whether the breeze
With soft, delicious murmur fans thy face,
Or water sleeps on thy white shoulders, these

Believe to be my love, which lends its grace
To all fair things, all feelings that may please
Thee, clasping thee for ever in its embrace.

Now and Always

NOW—: and with eyes that flashed, as fearing naught,
Stretched forth his hand from Nice her fair-haired son,
And, like a leopard on its prey, his thought
Leapt to achieve that which was to be done.

And always—: with fixed gaze the Genovan caught
The other's hand, austere in glance and tone,
And o'er the battle, which the heroes fought,
The Light of the Eternal Ideal shone.

Above earth's tumult soars the word of Faith
Through air serene with lofty visions, and cries
That Death and Fortune shall be conquered soon.

Now—through the heav'n Staglieno questioneth,
Always—Caprera in mid-sea replies:
Full o'er the Pantheon shines the guardian Moon.

CROSSING THE TUSCAN MAREMMA

SWEET country, whose wild loveliness sank deep
Into my being, inspired my proud free song,
Gave me a heart, where hate and love ne'er sleep,
One glimpse of thee—again my pulse beats strong.

The hills, that still their wonted outline keep,
I recognise again; the dreams, that long
Ago I dreamed, bid me half smile, half weep;
And youth's enchanted visions about me throng.

Ah, all I dreamed and all I loved was vain!
Run as I might, I never reached the goal:
And I shall fall to-morrow; yet once again

The clouds that o'er thy distant hill-tops roll,
Thy fields that glisten through the morning rain,
Whisper of peace unto my storm-tossed soul.

An Ancient Lament

THE tree to which my darling
Would point in childish wonder,
The green pomegranate yonder
With crimson blossoms bright,

Lone in the silent garden
The young green mantled o'er it,
E'en now doth June restore it
In summer warmth and light.

Thou of my stem the blossom,
This withered stem so stricken,
Thou, who my days didst quicken,
My one, my last delight,

In the cold earth thou hest,
In the black earth for ever;
Sunshine and love can never
For thee break winter's night.

WINTER WEARINESS

WERE there then roses once
On earth and violets bright?
Did the sun give warmth and light
From a smiling Heaven above?

Was there a golden Time
When all the world was young,
When youth and maiden sung
Of Valour, Faith, and Love?

Perchance such times there were,
Old poets have it so;
But that was long ago,
And no sun shines to-day.

And these unlovely fogs
By winter round me curled
Are the ashes of a world
That hath long since passed away.

PANTHEISM

YE wakeful stars, to you I never breathed it,
To thee, all-seeing sun, no whisper came:
About my heart in silence I enwreathed it,
That fairest flower of all things fair—her name.

Yet one star to another repeats my story,
When darkling night sheds down her welcome boon:
And lo, the great sun, when he sinks in glory,
Murmurs my secret to the silver moon.

The shady hills and joyful meadows know it,
'Tis told by every tree to every flower:
The birds fly past me singing: "Gloomy poet,
At length thou feelest love's enchanting power."

I never spake it, yet the earth and heaven
Shout her dear name in universal glee:
'Mid scents by blossoming acacias given
The world-soul whispers: "Thy love loveth thee."

ANACREONTICA ROMANTICA

'TWAS on a fair May morning
That I buried the God of Love:
O'er his grave the sun was shining,
An acacia bloomed above.

By all the birds of heaven
Was his mournful requiem sung,
And the tiny God was buried
The lilies and roses among:

Among the roses and lilies
Of my own beloved one's breast:
The meadows were red with flowers,
Heav'n smiled from east to west.

And a melancholy memory
Was set to guard his grave:
What more acceptable funeral
Could the little dead God have?

Yet, alas, his tomb's but a cradle
To a tiny bat-like thing!
For at nights when the moon is risen
Out from his grave he'll spring,

And on to my burning temples
With outstretched wings doth leap,
And he fans them gently, gently,
Till he makes me fall asleep.

To my weary spirit the murmur
Of trees and a brook comes back,
And I see a fair white forehead
Smile out from a veil of black.

And so while he holds me gently
In the fetters of sleep oppressed,
He bites me twice—in my temples,
All sweat-bedewed, and my breast.

Love sucks the warm red life-blood,
So softly I feel no pain:
But my life is fading slowly,
Fading from heart and brain.

To imprison this evil vampire
So that he trouble me not,
I must open the grave where I laid him,
And a priest must bless the spot.

Then shall the spell be broken,
And the dead corpse crumble to dust:
And never again shall the demon
In my life-blood sate his lust.

My dead Love's grave is thy bosom,
I will open it, lady fair:
For fain would mine eyes behold him,
The wee God, lying there.

That at last he be dust and ashes
I long to have some sure sign:
Disdain shall be my priest, dear,
And my holy water—wine.

A Morning Serenade

THE sun beats at thy lattice, "Rise, dear maiden,
'Tis time to love," saith he; "do I not make thee
Long for the breeze with violet perfumes laden,
Have I not bid the roses sing to wake thee?
April and May I bring from my resplendent
Kingdom to be on thee, their Queen, attendant,
And the new year lingers to pay his duty
And homage to the charms of thy young beauty."

The wind beats at thy lattice, "O'er the ocean,
O'er hill and plain," saith he, "where'er I travelled
The world to-day throbbed with but one emotion,
Living and dead in but one thought have revelled.
    The birds are singing and the bees are humming:
'Now let us love, love, love: for Spring is coming';
    And hark, the tombs decked with new flowers are sighing:
'Love, love, love while ye may: for Time is flying.'"

My thought beats at thy heart, which is a garden
Of lovely flowers, and asks one question only:
"May I come in and rest?" Oh, do not harden
Thy heart, for I am old and sad and lonely.
    I yearn to rest amid those happy flowers,
Dreaming a bliss that never yet was ours:
    I yearn to rest in peace and dream for ever
Of bliss which now may ne'er be mine—ah, never.

SAINT MARTIN

THE drizzling mist mounts slowly
And all the rough hills veileth;
Lashed by the north wind waileth
The sea, grey like the earth;

But through the suburb's alleys
A pungent scent from seething
Vats is wafted, breathing
Of wine and festal mirth.

Stands at his door the huntsman:
Within, the logs are blazing:
He stands and whistles, gazing,
While the spit turns on the hearth,

At dark bird-flocks migrating
Thro' the red-tinged clouds of even,
Like thoughts to exile driven
From the mind that gave them birth.

A Vision

LATE in the wintry skies the light-giver
Wan hosts of shadows was slowly o'erthrowing:
Down the long furrows, where tender blades shiver,
Green 'neath the sunbeams ploughlands were glowing.

Floating by smoothly ran Po's royal river,
Sparkling in sunlight the Mincio was flowing:
Then did my soul's white dream-pinions quiver
Oped toward a fantasy wondrously growing.

And in the mellow mild glory shining
From that calm *fata morgana* the early
Days of youth rose in my heart, dimly seen:

Rose without memories, without repining,
Like a green island that looms through a pearly
Haze in the distance far off and serene.

Springs of Hellas
(The Dorian)

KNOW'ST thou that island, which the Ionian laves,
And with his last most fragrant kisses thrills,
Where Galatea sports 'mid azure waves,
     And Acis haunts the hills?

Where on Pelasgian Eryx shady crest
Eternal Aphrodite rules above,
And all the radiant coast by her caressed
     Tingles and throbs with love?

Love, love, the meadows and the mountains sing,
When Enna's Maid from Hell she rendered sweet,
Returns to tearful Ceres with the Spring
     Burgeoning around her feet.

Love, love, the waters murmur; Arethuse
Hears once again Alpheus' wooing voice,
Who bids the Italian with the Grecian muse
     In one sweet strain rejoice.

Love, love The poets' songs in city walls
Are sung again; and, maddened with desire,
Through Doric forums dance wild Bacchanals,
     Flower-wreathed and with the lyre.

Not in my prayers stands towered Syracuse
Or Acragas, where Pindar's great song rings,
And full a hundred palms their shade diffuse
     Around the home of kings.

But say, where is that valley crowned with pine,
That lonely vale in the Nebrodian hills,
Where shepherd Daphnis sang his songs divine
     Among the sparkling rills?

"Oh, not for me to rule with princely sway
King Pelops' land, or hoard great store of gold,
Or dare outstrip the winds upon their way,
    In rivalry too bold.

"My dearest wish—on this bare crag to sing,
And while my arm, sweet maid, encircles thee,
To watch far off our white lambs pasturing
    By the Sicilian sea."

So sang the Dorian stripling debonair,
And nightingales were silent. To that shore,
O Argive soul, veiled in a veil as fair
    As Beatricë wore,

I'll snatch thee in my verse while at midday
The lazy meadow slumbers, and no sound
Breaks the bright stillness of each gulf and bay
    In sea and sky around,

From sunny hills I will the Dryads wake,
Dryads with golden hair and dancing feet;
And the old Gods of Homer I will make
    Come forth thy charms to greet.

Dead are the other gods: the deities
Of Greece know no decay in flowers they sleep,
In streams or mountains, in their native trees,
    Or in the eternal deep.

Before Christ's eyes all into marble froze,
Such was their pure and naked beauty's doom;
The poet, Lina, only the poet, knows
    Their never-ageing bloom.

And if the beauty that they love so well
Shine in a maiden's face or poet's lay,
From sacred Nature, answering that spell,
    Their smiles flash out alway.

See Dryads dancing and the Oread band!
"What age of man," they ask, "bore thee so fair?
Whence com'st thou, sister sweet, from what strange land,
          To breathe our lucent air?

"Deep sorrow overclouds thy starry eyes:
Say, hath the Cyprian dealt thee some fell blow?
All beauty, that with Aphrodite's vies,
          Finds her a cruel foe.

"Alone 'mong men could Helen conjure sleep,
And poured nepenthë in the heroes' wine,
But we know all the mysteries hidden deep
          In Gæa's bosom divine.

"And secret balsams we will pluck for thee,
For which enchanted mortals oft have wept,
And pearls by Amphitritë far at sea
          From human avarice kept.

"We'll gather for thee flowers, life-inspired,
Deep versed in every joy, in every woe,
And thou wilt of their stories ne'er be tired—
          Love-tales of long ago.

"They'll tell thee how the red rose doth despair,
Faint with desire upon thine ivory breast,
And how her proud white sister in thine hair
          Boasts she cloth love thee best.

"And thou shalt come with us to grottos bright
With crystal and with amethystine glow,
Where Forms and Elements in dance unite,
          While centuries onward flow.

"And we will bathe with thee in many a stream
Where sing white swans with all the Naiad brood,
Whose silvery sides upon the waters gleam
          Like moonlight on the flood.

"And thou shalt mount those heaven-kissing hills,
The best beloved of Zeus, our father, where
Apollo's lyre the Gods' high temple fills
    Athwart the throbbing air.

"There, gathered in our fragrant halls above,
The lovely Hylas shall be thine to wed
Hylas, for whom with wintry death we strove
    And won him from the dead."

Ah, since the setting of your golden day
Sorrow is born with men, and mars our peace!
Then grudge me not of love this one sole ray,
    Daughters of ancient Greece.

The unknown pain that gnaws her balmy breast
I'll purge with honey, pure as Hesiod's own;
I'll borrow Pindar's lyre to soothe to rest
    The grief that makes her moan.

Were I Alceus, her gentle form should glow
Transfigured in the glory of my odes;
I'd wreathe her locks with deathless flowers that grow
    To crown the brows of Gods.

I'd prop her on a fragrant purple couch
Of hyacinth beneath my laurel-tree,
And murmur as I bent her lips to touch:
    "Sweet lady, I love thee."

RECOLLECTIONS OF SCHOOL

IT was mid-June, upon a lovely day
Of pulsing Messidor, and like a bride
The earth glowed 'neath the kisses of the sun,
Who with a fiery torrent overflowed
The desert spaces of the shining heav'n,
And at his smile divine the ocean laughed.
But I, the boy, laughed not: a black-gowned priest
In accents hoarse was blaspheming *amo*.
How tedious was his face! Meanwhile against
The window of the school a cherry-tree
Pushed boldly up, and with his bright red fruit
Winked joyously, and whispered with the breeze
Strange, secret stories. Whence I soon forgot
The priest and the long rows of conjugations
That crawled across the yellow page like ants
Upon grey chalk, and to my heart's desire
I yielded, and set free my eyes and thoughts
To wander through the window: on this side
I saw the sky and mountains, and on that
A distant curving line of sea. The birds
Singing in thousand choirs flew here and there
Through sunlit heav'ns: unto the twittering nests
The ancient trees, like pious guardians, seemed
To speak, and to the buzzing bees the shrubs,
And for the kisses of the butterflies
The flowers seemed sighing: stems and grass and reeds
Swarmed with the murmurous hum of life and love,
A thousand thousand little lives that breathed
At every moment. And the mountains dark
And the serene hills and the rippling fields
Of corn, 'mid yellowing vineyards and green woods,
And last the prickly thickets and the briars
And livid marshland, all seemed to rejoice
In everlasting youth beneath the sun.
When, how I know not, as if from the fount
Of life itself sprang up within my heart
The thought of death, and with death came the thought
Of nothingness: and suddenly, when I

Compared the infinite sense of feeling all
With that of feeling naught, and seeing myself
Bodily in the black earth, silent, cold,
And motionless, while joyously without
The birds were piping, trees were whispering,
The rivers flowing, and all living things
Renewed themselves in the warm sun, whose light
Divine flowed round them, did I realise
The whole, the full, significance of death,
And was in sooth appalled. Even to-day
That boyish fancy, when it rises up
Within my memory, like a sudden jet
Of icy water, overwhelms my heart.

An Idyll of the Maremma

STILL when young April's rosy light doth shine
Into my room, thy sudden smile can move,
O fair-haired Mary, this sad heart of mine:

This heart, to which long years of struggle prove
How sweet were rest with thee whom it forgot,
O my first love, sweet dawn of my first love!

Where art thou? Not forlorn thou sighest, not
Unwed: thy native village bath for sure
In thee a joyous bride and mother got;

Too rich in promise to a husband's pure
Embrace was that young form, that heaving breast,
Which its confining veil could scarce endure.

Surely strong sons were to thy bosom pressed,
Who now leap on their steeds of mettle keen,
With loving glances unto thee addressed.

How lovely wart thou, maiden, as between
The swell of the long furrows, with a wreath
Of wild flowers in thy hand, myself have seen

Thee, tall and smiling, come, the while beneath
Thy vivid brows the large blue- eyes profound
Would unto me one bright, shy glance bequeath.

For like the cornflower 'twixt the wheatstalks found
Blooming serene, 'neath tangled golden hair
Shone thy blue eyes: before thee and around

Flamed the vast summer: in the sunlit air
The green pomegranate branches swayed, where gleamed
The red fruit 'mid the foliage here and there.

The gorgeous peacock at thy passing seemed
To greet its queen, spreading, all azure-eyed,
Its tail, and gazing at thee harshly screamed.

How chill my life seems now when set beside
Those happy days, how dark, how wearisome!
'Twere better, dear, to have made thee my bride!

Better thro' pathless bush go tracking some
Driv'n buffalo, which in the copse will wait
And gaze, then rush on when pursuers come,

Than after petty, paltry rhymes to sweat!
Better by work to have forgot, than sought
To solve, vast riddles that no man solved yet!

Now cold, remorseless, doth the worm of thought
Gnaw through my brains, whence in my bitter pain
I write and speak sad words with misery fraught.

With heart and muscles wasted through the strain
Of mind self-tortured, bones all festering
From civil ruin, I madly writhe in vain.

Oh, the long lines of poplars .whispering
Unto the breeze! Oh, in the cool shade, nigh
The little chapel, on fête-days the ring

Of rustic seats, where brown the ploughlands lie
Below, and green the hills, yon sea with white
Sails dotted, and the old graveyard close by!

Oh, sweet the talk with comrades in the bright,
Still noontide, sweet the cosy gathering late
Around the hearth upon a winter's night!

Oh, glorious, far more glorious, to relate
To eager youngsters tales of derring-do,
The hard-fought chase, the dangers that await

The huntsman, and with finger trace anew
The slanting wounds on the prone wild-boar seen,
Than with a pack of lying rhymes pursue

The cowards of Italy and Trissottin.

CLASSICISM AND ROMANTICISM

KIND is the sun: man's work he doth not scorn:
    His beams are warm and blithe:
Through him the rustling leagues of golden corn
    Bow to the reaper's scythe.

He laughs to see the ploughshare cleave the brown,
    Rich clods asunder, till
The damp steel glitters, while the ox moves down
    The slowly furrowed hill.

He gilds with fiery hues the swelling grape
    By vine-leaves veiled from sight;
Nor do late autumn's drunken revels escape
    His milder, wintrier light.

His ray doth pierce through city smoke and murk
    The grimy roofs among,
Unto the poor girl, who, worn out by work,
    Forgets that she is young,

Bidding her in the glad springtime rejoice.
    Her bosom throbs, and hark,
Warmed by his cheerful light, her heart and voice
    Soar upward like the lark.

But thou, moon, lov'st to silver with thy ray
    Old ruins and scenes of woe;
Nor flowers nor fruit on thy fantastic way
    To ripen dost thou know.

Where Hunger sleeps in darkness thy light steals
    Soft thro' the window chinks,
And wakens him, so that the cold he feels
    And of the morrow thinks.

On Gothic spires dost thou thyself adorn,
   Milk-white and motionless
Day-weary poets and silly folk lovelorn
   Thy fickle beams caress.

Then to the graveyard: proudly dost thou there
   Refresh thy weary light,
Boasting that skulls and bones, how white so'er,
   As thou, are not so white.

I hate thee, with thy starched white cotta on,
   Round-faced stupidity,
Unfruitful and lascivious little nun,
   Sky-sister of charity.

Before San Guido

THE cypresses, which still to Bólgheri run stately
And tall from San Guido in a double file,
Like a band of youthful giants, came, sedately
Bowing, to meet me, and gazed at me awhile.

Soon they recognised me, and their tall heads bending,
"So you have returned," softly murmured they;
"Why not stay here, your weary journey ending?
For the eve is cool, and well you know the way.

"Oh, sit you here, our fragrant boughs above you,
Where the west wind from the sea your cheek can touch!
Spite of the stones you used to throw at us we love you
Just the same as ever; oh, they never hurt us much.

"Why rush on so quickly when you hear us crying?
The nightingale still in our branches builds his nest;
Still may you see the sparrows round us flying
In the gathering twilight. Oh, stay with us and rest!"

"Darling little cypresses, cypresses beloved,
In happy bygone days the truest friends I had,"
Gazing, I answered, I hear you not unmovèd:
How glad would I be to stay with you—how glad!

"But, cypresses, old comrades, that chapter is completed:
Boyhood's days are over: you must let me go I
Have you never heard?—well, think me not conceited,
But—I am to-day a celebrity, you know.

"Greek I can read, in Latin I am fluent,
My mind is stored with knowledge, and I write and write:
O cypresses, from school I no longer play the truant,
No longer throw stones, for I should not deem it right—

"Not at trees at least." Thro' all the tree-tops rocking,
As doubting of my answer, a murmur seemed to run,
And their dark green depths flushed rosy with a mocking
Radiance cast upon them by the setting sun.

Ah, then I knew I was gazed on with compassion
By the sun and cypresses, and I soon began
To hear words mingle with the murmur in this fashion:
"Yes, we knew it well: you're a poor deluded man.

"Yes, we knew it welly for the wind, who is so clever
At catching mortals' sighs, has told us all the truth,
How within your breast conflicting passions ever
Burn, which you cannot and know not how to soothe.

"Here to the oaks and to us you may at leisure
Recount your human sadness, all the woes of men.
Peaceful lies the ocean, one sheet of living azure,
Smiling the sun dips down to it again.

"See how the birds thro' the dusk their flight are winging!
The sparrows twitter cheerfully, now the day is done;
At nightfall you shall hear the nightingales singing:
Rest, and bid the evil phantoms all begone!

"Those evil phantoms, raised by gloomy fancies
From the heart's black depths, which confuse your way,
Like a will-o'-the-wisp that in a graveyard dances
Before the traveller's eyes, leading him astray.

"Rest, and to-morrow, when the sun is high in heaven,
When in the oak-tree shade the horses meet,
And all around you the silent plain is given
Up to noonday slumber in the shimmering heat,

"We will bid the murmuring, breezes softly kiss you,
Which make eternal music 'twixt the earth and sky:
Forth from the elm-trees there the nymphs shall issue
And with their white veils fan you dreamily:

"And Pan, the eternal, who wanders solitary,
   On the heights at noonday or through the lonely plain
The discord, O mortal, of your cares shall bury
   In harmony divine, and give you peace again."

And I: "Far away across the mountains yonder
   My Titti, my daughter, is waiting: let me go!
Sparrow-like she may be, but you must not wonder
   If her little frocks do not, like feathers, grow.

"Nor will cypress berries her tiny body fatten:
   Whilst I 'gainst the methods of Manzonians rebel,
Who each on the produce of four salaries batten:
   Farewell, my cypresses! Sweet Tuscan plain, farewell

"To the graveyard then must we bear your sad confession,
   Where your Granny lieth?" And they flitted past,
Seeming like a black funereal procession,
   Muttering as they hastened ever faster and more fast.

Then on the hill-top from the cemetery,
   Coming down the green path, again I seemed to see a
Figure 'neath the cypresses, very tall and very
   Stately, dressed in black, my grandmother Lucia.

The lady Lucia, with silver tresses plaited
   Neatly o'er her forehead, how softly she could croon
The Tuscan dialect, not the emasculated
   Manzonian jargon of the Florentine buffoon.

The pure Versilian accent from her lips descended
   With a mournful music, that still my memory haunts,
All its strength and sweetness exquisitely blended
   Like the *sirventesi* sung in old Provence.

Oh, Granny, Granny, I thought it all so pretty
   When I was a baby! Oh, tell it me again;
Tell this man grown worldly-wise the ancient ditty
   Of her who sought her lost love thro' the world in vain.

"I have worn to nothing in my weary going
Seven pairs of iron shoes that naught could break:
I have worn out seven staves of iron, bowing
My tired body o'er them, while search for thee I make.

"Seven flasks of tears have I filled to overflowing
In seven years of bitter weeping for thy sake;
Yet thou sleepest on, and the cock is crowing:
Deaf to my despairing cries, thou wilt not wake."

Granny, how pretty and how true the tale appears
Even now to me! Why, it is exactly so!
And that which I have sought thro' so many, many years
From sunrise to sunset perhaps is here, below

These cypresses, where now I can never hope to wander,
Never dream again of resting in the shade:
It is perhaps, Granny, in the cemetery yonder,
'Mid those other cypresses up there, where you are laid.

Panting the train swept onward, never staying,
While in my heart I wept thus bitterly;
And a troop of young colts galloped towards us neighing
Joyously, the cause of all the din to see.

But an old grey donkey, who on a purple thistle
Was grazing close beside me, seemed no interest to feel;
Never deigned to look when he heard the engine whistle,
But gravely and slowly proceeded with his meal.

ON MARENGO'S PLAINS
THE NIGHT OF EASTER EVE IN THE YEAR 1175

ON Marengo's plains is beating the moonlight: dark between
The Bormida and Tanaro a forest, dimly seen,
Tosses and moans—a forest of halberds, steeds, and men,
Fleeing from Alexandria, from the ramparts stormed in vain.

Lo, Alexandria's watch-fires down, down from Apennine
On the dreadful rout and ruin of the Ghibelline Emperor shine;
From Tortona flash the watch-fires of the League their answering light,
And a song of triumph echoes through the calm and gracious night.

"Trapped lies the Swabian tyrant, the Lion of the North,
By Latin swords! To hills and seas, O watch-fires, flash it forth!
To-morrow is Christ's Easter; and ere to-morrow's done
How gloriously shall triumph the Roman folk, O Sun!"

The white-haired Hohenzollern hears that exultant cry;
With head bowed o'er his mighty sword he ponders: "Must we die
At the hand of these base traders, who but yesterday did dare
To gird round their sleek bellies swords only knights may wear?"

And Speier's lordly prelate, whose bursting wine-butts store
The fruit of five-score vales, whose stalls hold canons full five-score,
Bemoans: "O stately towers of my own cathedral shrine,
Within ye who on Christmas Eve shall chant the Mass divine?"

And Detpold, Count of Palatine, whose golden tresses stream
Adown his slender neck, whereon the rose and lily gleam, Thinks:
"Thro' the dark go singing the pixies of the Rhine,
While my little Thekla slumbers beneath the white moonshine."

His Grace the Lord Archbishop of Mayence groans: "I bear
By my steel mace the sacred oil: therein all men may share;
But, oh, that yonder sumpter-mules, each with its precious load
Of Italian silver, were at least safe up the Alpine road!"

And the Count of Tyrol murmurs: "My son, to-morrow's dawn
On Alpine heights shall greet thee, on thee my hound shall fawn.
Thine are they both: thy father, like stag by village swains
Entrapped, shall fall with severed throat on these grey Lombard plains."

Alone within the middle of the camp, his charger nigh,
The Emperor stood gazing up at the midnight sky:
O'er his grey head were passing the silent stars; behind,
The Banner of the Empire hung flapping in the wind.

On either flank Bohemia's and Poland's monarchs wait:
Two warrior-kings, twin pillars of the Holy Roman State.
When the stars grew dim and weary, when the Alpine summits shone
Rose-red at dawn, then haughtily Cæsar commands: 'March on!'

"To horse, ye loyal vassals! Thou, Wittelsbach, display
Our sacred standard in the eyes of the Lombard League this day!
Herald, go shout: 'The Roman Cæsar doth pass, divine
Heir of the godlike Julius, of Trajan's royal line!'"

How rapidly, how joyously the German bugles blow
From regiment to regiment 'twixt Tanaro and Po,
When in the Eagle's presence th' Italian vassals cast
Their courage from them and bent low in awe—while Cæsar passed!

To Victor Hugo
(27th February 1881)

FROM mountains at the touch of rosy-fingered morning glowing
The epic verse of Homer like a stream divine is flowing,
By white swans haunted, through the fertile Asiatic plain.
      The tragedy of Aeschylus arises, rough and splendid
'Mid horror of fate and roar of fire and smoke and thunder blended,
Like Etna in the night-time o'er the dark Sicilian main.

The Olympic ode of Pindar, with oarage of its pinions
Like an eagle soaring proudly in its own supreme dominions,
Floats triumphantly at midday over mart and town beneath.
      In my study stands thy statue, grey-haired Victor Hugo, near
To the books of these three poets, with thy forehead of a seer
On thy right hand propped, as seeming one whom grief o'er-burdeneth.

Dost dream of sons or country? Dost dream of human sorrow?
I know not; but when, O prophet, of that secret grief I borrow
      A spell for heart and eyes,
No memory of losses past or present loss abideth,
But I remember years that were, and those the future hideth,
      And that which never dies.
I placed upon thy brow a twig of laurel, for thee broken
From off a nameless tomb beside the Appian Way, as token
      How I thy genius prize.
Poet, thou wert o'er force of Fate and Circumstance victorious;
Poet, beneath thy shining foot the Emperor inglorious
      With all his Empire lies.

What carest thou for life? Who tells the years thou shalt inherit?
Thou art of Gaul, thou art of France the everlasting spirit,
Which bursts from thy great heart to take its flight through centuries.
      In thee the muttering storms athwart the Breton sand-dunes
        creeping,
In thee the dreams of Norman plains beneath the moonlight sleeping,
In thee the heat of granite cliffs of the sunny Pyrenees.

In thee the sunburnt health of Bourgogne's vintagers, the fire
Of that Provencal song whose note Greek harmonies inspire,
The genius of the soil where Marne and Seine encircling flow.
        Thou sawest the Nomad wains encamped where once great
            Ilium towered,
Heard'st Frankish Roland wind his horn in Roncivalle o'er-powered,
Did'st talk familiarly with Godfrey, Bayard, and Marceau.

Thy fateful work, like Druid oak, a dreadful awe diffuses,
Whose sacred mistletoe is cut with golden axe by Muses
        Clad in white draperies.
From sunlit branches hang the harps; which bards of old have sounded,
Hang the ancestral arms; but nightingales within the rounded
        Shields sing love-melodies.
Spring whispers thro' the leaves, and girls deep in the shade are dancing.
And little children, golden-curled, with great blue eyes up glancing
        Toward the evening skies,
Where the tall branches mingle with the twilight, gaze in wonder,
For thither pass, girt round with lightning-flash and roar of thunder,
        The avenging Deities.

Poet, I've hung the tricolour upon thy tresses hoary,
Sent to me from the Danube, from the waters of Salvore
By Trieste, who to none in passionate love of Rome doth yield.
        Poet, from the wall that faces thee the Brescian Victory crieth:
"What year resplendent with the light of a fame that never dieth,
What name, shall I inscribe upon my everlasting shield?"

Our glories pass like churchyard wraiths that morning sunbeams banish,
Like shifting scenery of the stage kingdoms and empires vanish, Yet
archangelic moves thy-verse serene and proud and free.
        To coming ages sing, old man, in godlike exultation
The "Carmen Seculare" of the great Latin nation:
Yea, sing to the expectant world, Justice and Liberty.

The King of Thule
(From the Ballads of W. Goethe)

THERE was a king in Thule
   Right loyal to the grave,
To whom his dying ladye
   A golden goblet gave.

Naught valued he above it,
   He drained it every bout:
He wept, so did he love it,
   When'er he drank thereout.

And when death called this lover
   He reckoned town and pelf,
To heirs all handed over,
   All, save the goblet's self.

He called to his royal table
   His knights, then down sate he
In his castle, high and stable,
   Above the restless sea.

Rose that old toper: slowly
   He quaffed his life's last glow,
Then hurled the goblet holy
   Far in the flood below.

He watched it falling, filling,
   Sinking deep in the sea:
To close his eyes now willing,
   Ne'er another drop drank he.

THE POET

FOLK profane, I'd have ye know it
That the poet
Is no merry-andrew, able
By his vulgar tricks to waste the
Bread and taste the
Dainties at another's table.

And still less is he a lazy
Fool, in hazy
Day-dreams wrapt, for ever spying
After angels, head in air
In despair
To see naught but martins flying.

Nor is he a garden lover,
Such as over
Life's path scatters with the spade his
Rich manure, and men-folk dowers
With cabbage flowers,
Keeping violets for the ladies.

The poet is a mighty blacksmith,
Whose broad back 's with
Iron muscles furrowed: daily
He, with pride of strength invested,
Works, bare-chested,
Sinewy-armed, and smiling gaily.

Ere the twitter of birds gives warning
Of glad morning
On the hill hath he descended,
And with roaring bellows wakes the
Flame that makes the
Forge, whereat he labours, splendid.

And the firelight boldly dances,
Sparkles, glances,
Glowing red with rosy flashes;
Then it hisseth, then it roareth,
Then it soareth
Upward, crackling from the ashes.

God, who smiles upon the poet,
Knows—for know it
I do not—the art wherewith the
Eager smith wists how to throw in
To the glowing
Flames, which light his wondrous smithy,

Love and thought, pure as pure ore is,
All the glories
Of his nation and his fathers.
Past and Future in one shining
Mass combining
He within his furnace gathers.

Then he grips the mass and holds it
While he moulds it
On the anvil, singing ever
As he hammers. And the sunrise
Glows upon his
Brow and rude toil, ceasing never.

He hammers! Lo, when Freedom charges,
Swords and targes
For her valiant warriors welded!
Lo, wreaths destined for victorious
Heroes, glorious
Crowns to Queens of Beauty yielded.

He hammers! Lo, rich sanctuaries
For the Lares
And their age-long rites intended!
Tripods lo, and altar-pieces
Lo, rare friezes,
Massy goblets rich and splendid.

For himself the poor smith taketh
Gold, and maketh
Thence a shaft, and shoots it sunward,
Asking but to watch it flying
Radiant, high in
Heaven, ever upward, onward.

from
ODI BARBARE

Schlechten gestümperten Versen genügt ein geringer Gehalt schon
  Während die edlere Form tiefe Gedanken bedarf:
Wollte man euer Geschwätz ausprägen zur sapphischen Ode,
  Würde die Welt einsehn, dass es ein leeres Geschwätz.

AUGUST V. PLATEN.

Musa latina, vieni meco a canzone novella:
  Può nuova progenie it canto novello fare.

T. CAMPANELLA.

PRELUDE

I HATE the common muse: she lies
    With languid limbs and yields her charms
Without one struggle, an easy prize
    To any vulgar lover's arms.

For me the watchful "Strophe's" beat
    Of dancing foot in rhythmic choir!
I grasp her, as she spreads her fleet
    Wings to escape, nor heed her ire.

So writhes on Haemus' snowy height
    Some Eviad in a Faun's embrace,
Who finds her lovelier, as more tight
    Her panting breast his arms enlace,

And on her burning lips his kiss
    Smothers the shriek: in sunlight gleams
Her brow, that white as marble is,
    While down the wind her long hair streams.

THE IDEAL

SWEET perfumes of ambrosia rise
  From thy full cup and drown my sense,
  O Hebe Goddess, passing hence
In radiant flight with smiling eyes.

No more I feel the chilling pains
  Of gloomy age, with sorrow rife,
  O Hebe, but I feel the life
Of Hellas coursing through my veins.

The ruined days that strew the slope
  Of my dark past rose up once more,
  O Hebe, pleading to restore
Themselves in thy sweet light of Hope.

And the new years, like mountain heights
  That catch the day, while all below
  Is dark, O Hebe, blush and glow,
Illumined by thy rosy lights.

Bright star, thou with thy radiant fires
  On days and years alike dost shine
  From Heaven; as, in some Gothic shrine
High over all the climbing spires

Of marble black and white, upon
  The topmost pinnacle doth stand
  Jesse's sweet daughter, calm and grand
And glistening like a golden sun;

On Champaign seamed with silver streaks
  Of winding river she gazes down,
  On waving corn and distant town
And gleaming snow on Alpine peaks.

Though drifting clouds enwrap her, yet
  Her shining face smiles through the mist
  When dawning May the earth hath kissed
And sad November suns are set.

On the Anniversary of the Foundation of Rome

THEE April's flowers beheld, when first
From Romulus's furrow burst
    Thy battlements and frowned
    On the wild plains around:

Thee, worn by centuries of time,
The April sun still greets, sublime
    And great, our age-long home,
    Flower of Italy, Rome.

Tho' down the sacred way the four
White steeds in triumph pass no more,
    Tho' no High Priest climb now
    The Capitol's steep brow

With silent Vestal, yet, more grand,
Thy Forum's lonely ruins stand;
    Strength, order, peace 'mong men
    Are Roman now as then.

Hail, Rome divine I That man who knows
Thee not cold mists of night enclose;
    In his base heart a crop
    Of barbarous weeds springs up.

Hail, Rome divine! With bowed, sad face
Thy Forum's stones I love to trace,
    Kissing each broken sign
    Of thee, our Mother divine.

By thee, I'm poet, great Nurse of men,
By thee, Italian citizen.
    The world wakes at thy name,
    Thou gav'st to Italy fame.

To thee returns this Italy
Thou madest one, thou madest free.
   Lo, on thy breast she lies,
   Drawn by thine eagle eyes.

From silent Forum, storied hill
Stretch forth thy marble arms, and still
   To her who frees thee show
   Arches and columns now

Awaiting no new triumphings
Of Cæsars and victorious kings,
   With captives ta'en in war
   Bound to their ivory car,

Nay, but your triumph, Italian folk,
O'er monstrous Powers and their fell yoke
   Whence with calm justice ye
   Shall set all nations free.

Italy, Rome! That day shall cries
Of glory, glory, glory rise
   Above the Forum through
   Th' unclouded thund'ring blue.

By the Sources of Clitumnus

STILL, Clitumnus, down from the mountain, dark with
Waving ash-trees, where 'mid the branches perfumed
Breezes whisper, wafting afar the scent of
Wild-thyme and wood-sage,

Still descend the flocks in the misty ev'ning
Unto thee; and still do the boys of Umbria
Dip the struggling sheep in thy gleaming waters,
While from the bosom

Of the sunburnt mother, who sits barefooted
By her cottage singing, the smiling baby
Turns towards his brothers his chubby features
Radiant with laughter;

And the father, wrapped in his shaggy goatskins
Like the Fauns of old, doth direct with thoughtful
Gaze the painted waggon and team of sturdy,
Beautiful oxen:

Beauteous oxen, massive of shoulder, mild-eyed,
White as snow, with horns that above their foreheads
Curve like crescent moons, such as gentle Virgil
Loved for their beauty.

Even now, like columns of smoke, the clouds rise
Dark o'er Apennine: 'mid her zone of gently
Sloping hills how lovely, austere, and verdant
Umbria lieth!

Hail, green land of Umbria I hail, pure fountain,
God Clitumnus, hail! In my heart I feel the
Ancient Fatherland, and my fevered forehead
Brushed by the pinions

Of th' Italian Deities. Who bath darkened
This, thy hallowed stream, with the weeping willow?
May the wind, degenerate tree, uproot thee,
Hateful to heroes.

Here let holm-oaks battle with winter, murmur
When the earth is throbbing with spring their secret
Stories—holm-oaks black and o'ergrown with gay green
Garlands of ivy.

Here, like giant sentinels round the rising
God, let lofty cypresses crowd to hide him;
Chant thou then thine oracles, O Clitumnus,
Veiled in their shadow.

Tell us, O thou witness of three great empires,
How the stubborn Umbrian, fiercely fighting,
Sank 'neath Velite lances, how strong Etruria
Grew ever stronger:

Tell how then Gradivus descended swiftly
On the twelve confederate cities, leaving
Conquered Mount Ciminius, how he planted
Rome's haughty standards.

Yet did'st thou, th' indigenous native Godhead,
Reconcile the conquerors and the conquered
When from Trasimene Carthaginian fury
Thundered towards Rome.

Then arose a cry from thy caverns, then the
Twisted horn woke echoes among the mountains:
"Ye that in the gloomy Mevanian hollow
Pasture fat oxen;

"Ye that by the banks of the Nar to leftward
Plough the slopes, and ye that cut down the copses
O'er Spoleto; ye that in Martian Todi
Celebrate nuptials,

"Leave the full-fed ox in the rushes, leave the
Tawny bull to stand in mid-furrow, leave the
Wedge stuck fast in tottering oak-tree, leave the
Bride at the altar:

"Run ye, run ye, run ye with axe and javelin
Run with spears, with bludgeons, and fresh-cut lances
Run, your household gods to defend from dreadful
Hannibal's onslaught!"

Ah, how fair it shone in the gracious sunlight
This retreat encircled by lovely mountains,
When Spoleto's citadel saw the shrieking
Rout of those ruthless

Moorish hordes, Numidian horses, mingled
All in horrid carnage, and o'er them hurtling
Steel, and burning rivers of oil, and thundrous
Shouts of the victors.

All is silent now. I can watch the tiny
Thread that gushes up thro' the smooth, clear eddies;
Watch it sway and stamp little bubbles on the
Mirror-like surface.

Deep below a miniature forest slumbers
Motionless, with branches together woven:
Amethyst and jasper in loving curves of
Beauty seem mingled.

And the flowers seem tinged with the hue of sapphire,
Flashing back a sparkle of diamond brilliance,
Radiant, cool, inviting me down to green, deep,
Silent abysses.

On the hills, by streams, in the shade of oak-trees
Seek the springs of Poetry, O my country!
Nymphs have lived, have lived: and this is indeed a
God's marriage-chamber.

Azure Naiads rose from the water, dimly
Seen thro' flowing veils: in the windless twilight
Came they, loudly calling their brown-haired sisters
Down from the mountains.

'Neath the moon, that hung like a lamp in heaven,
Wove they dances, chanting in joyful chorus
Of eternal Janus: how love o'ercame him,
Love for Camesna.

He from Heav'n, autochthonous, manlike, virgin
She: the misty Apennine was her bride-bed:
Clouds concealed that wondrous embrace, whose fruit was
Italy's people.

All is silent now, O bereaved Clitumnus,
All: and only one of thy lovely temples
Now remains, yet thou art no more enthroned there,
Toga-clad, awful.

Now no longer, sprinkled with holy water,
Bullocks proudly bear to the altar Roman
Trophies: fall'n the shrines of our fathers: Rome now
Triumphs no longer,

Triumphed nevermore, from the day when first that
Red-haired Galilean the Capitolian
Heights ascended, threw her his cross, and bad her
"Bear it and serve Me."

Fled the nymphs dismayed to their fountains weeping,
Or within the sheltering tree-trunks vanished:
Shrieking, all the Oreads melted, like the
Mist on the mountains,

When a weird black company through the ruined
Marble shrines and fall'n colonnades came chanting
Mournful psalms and litanies, slowly pacing,
Clothed in dark sackcloth.

And of plains resounding with human labour,
Hills that once imperial glories witnessed;
Made a dreadful desert, and called the, desert
"Kingdom of Heaven."

Multitudes were torn from the sacred ploughshare,
Torn from girlish brides and from aged parents;
All that ever basked in the blessed sunlight
Banning with curses,

Cursing all the business of life, nay, cursing
Very Love, they raved of repulsive unions,
Agony and pain with their God on lonely
Rocks and in caverns;

Then descending, frenzied with self-wrought ruin,
Citywards, fear-smitten, would dance and beg the
Crucifix with impious prayer that men might
Scorn and reject them.

Hail, O Human Spirit, serenely dwelling
On Ilissus' banks, and by Tiber's gracious
Shores enshrined as Justice, the night is over:
Rise again, rule us.

Thou, too, pious mother of matchless bullocks
Strong to break the glebe and upturn the fallow,
And of neighing steeds that delight in battle,
Italy mother,

Thou of corn and vines and of everlasting
Laws and arts far-famed, civilising nations,
Mother, hail! for thee I renew the ancient
Songs to extol thee.

Mountain, wood, and stream of this verdant Umbria
Shout applause; before us in smoke and thunder,
Herald of new industries, rusheth onward,
Shrieking, the engine.

IN A GOTHIC CATHEDRAL

RISING straightly, extend in their symmetrical,
Clean-cut lines these immense columns; mysteriously
Loom they, giantlike, huge, through the dim atmosphere,
Like some silent Titanic host

Plotting war in the night 'gainst the Invisible:
Arches noiselessly leap forth from the capitals,
Swiftly soar o'er the void, then to each other lean,
Poised in dizzy embrace on high.

So 'mid discord of men, 'mid the barbarian
Tumults, rose unto God sighs, supplications, tears,
Shed by downtrodden men, yearning in solitude
To unite themselves unto Him.

No God ask I from you, arches aerial,
Marble columns! I watch trembling to hear a light
Footfall, known unto me, which in its coming the
Solemn echoes awakeneth.

It is Lydia—she turns: lo, as she turns, her hair
Glimmers faint thro' the gloom, and for an instant the
Pale, sweet countenance smiles out from the veil of black,
Smiles out radiant with love to me.

He too, Dante of old, once in the dubious
Twilight stood of a vast Gothic cathedral, and
Sought with fear after God, finding Him in the pale,
Pearl-like gleam of a woman's face.

Clear beneath the white veil glimmered the maiden's brow;
All transfigured she shone, rapt in an ecstasy:
Incense drifted in clouds o'er her, and through the dim
Air rose passionate litanies;

Rose with murmured appeal, soft as a turtle-dove's
Low-breathed cooing they rose joyously heavenward,
Changing soon to the shrill wail of despairing throngs,
Who stretch hands of prayer forth to God.

O'er them weirdly the deep organ from arch to arch
Sobbed and sighed thro' the vast gloom: in the marble vaults
Far beneath them the dead bones of their ancestors
Seemed to whisper in sympathy.

But from Fiesole's height famous in history,
'Mid fair legends of saints, rosily through the panes
Gazed Apollo: the wax candles around the high
Altar paled and grew tremulous.

Dante saw 'mid the hymns chanted by angels his
Tuscan virgin ascend, saw in a vision her
Form transfigured, and heard how the abyss of Hell
Bellowed lurid beneath his feet.

Yet no demons see I, no, nor angelical
Light; I see but a flash, brilliant as lightning, that
Trembles through the damp air: twilight enwraps the soul
With grey mists and with weariness.

Lo, I bid thee farewell, dreadful Semitic God
O'er thy mysteries Death holdeth dominion.
Inaccessible King, ghosts are thy subjects, and
Thy dark temples exclude the sun.

Thou dost crucify men, crucified Deity!
Thou with sadness the pure air dost contaminate!
Yet the heaven is bright, yet are the meadows green,
Yet with love-lights are flashing the

Eyes of Lydia. I yearn, Lydia, to see thee with
White-robed virginal choirs dance in Apollo's praise
Round his altar, as day dies and the westering
Sun stains rosy its Parian

Stone till gemlike it glows red 'mid the laurel-trees.
Oh, to witness thee then scatt'ring anemones,
Flashing joy from thine eyes, singing in harmony
Some sweet hymn of Bacchylides!

SIRMIO

LO, on the shining lake green Sirmio glows like a jewel,
The flower of all peninsulas,

Gazed at, caressed by the sun: like a mighty goblet of silver,
Benacus wide encircles it.

Fringed are the gleaming shores with quiet olives and copses
Of everlasting laurel-trees.

This is the radiant cup by Mother Italy proffered
With arms uplifted to the Gods;

And from high heaven the Gods let Sirmio drop on the water,
The gem of all peninsulas.

Lovely she is; and Baldo, yon fatherly mountain, protects her
With stormy eyebrows from above:

Mongü lies like a fallen Titan, her champion in battle;
Supine he lies, yet threatening still.

Over against him Salò from her moon-shaped gulf to the leftward
Extends her white arms o'er the lake,

E'en as a blithesome maiden that enters the dance and abandons
Her veil and tresses to the wind,

Laughingly scattering handfuls of flowers, adorning with flowers
Her maiden brow exultantly.

Yonder below lifts Garda her gloomy rock o'er the water
Extended mirror-like beneath,

Chanting a saga of ancient towns long buried and vanished,
And tales of fair barbarian queens.

Nay, but, Lalage, here, whence the bountiful spaces of azure
Entrance thine eyes and soothe thy soul,

Here did Valerius Catullus below on the glistening pebbles Once
moor his swift Bithynian bark;

Here hath he sat long days, and Lesbia's eyes in the water
Phosphorescent and tremulous,

Yea, and Lesbia's treacherous smile and numberless graces, Hath
gazed at in the glassy flood,

While in the gloomy alleys of Rome fair Lesbia languished Among
the sons of Romulus.

Then from those liquid depths the lake-nymph called to him,
 singing:
"Come, O Quintus Valerius!

"Here, too, our grottos are bright with the sun, but diffused are
    the sunbeams
 Silvery soft like Cynthia's.

"Here Both the ceaseless roar of your life sink low, till it seemeth
A far-off murmur as of bees.

"Madness and fretful care are soothed in the cool and the silence,
And fade in slow forgetfulness.

"Sweet is it here to slumber while softly the musical chorus
Of azure virgins charms the ear,

"While pure Hesperus lengthens his rosy torch on the water
And wavelets sob upon the beach.'

Ah, sad Love! He hateth the Muses, and wantonly tortures
All poets with tragic cruelty.

And yet, who from thine eyes and thy warfare of amorous glances
Can feel secure, my Lalage?

Pluck for the stainless Muses three boughs of laurel and myrtle,
And wave them to th' eternal Sun.

Seëst thou not the flocks of white swans float from Peschiera
Adown the silv'ry Mincio?

Hearest thou not from the verdant meadows, where sleepeth Bianor,
The sound of Roman Virgil's voice?

Lalage, turn and adore! From the Scaligers' tower above thee
Looks forth a face austere and grand:

"Up in beautiful Italy—" smiling he murmurs, and gazes
On waters, earth, and azure air.

ON THE DEATH OF NAPOLEON EUGENE
(PRINCE IMPERIAL)

THIS one th' unknowing barbarous assegai
Laid low, and quenched the light of his eyes, which shone
Enraptured at the splendid visions
Bright thro' the limitless azure floating.

The other, with kisses sated, on Austrian
Cushions reclined, and dreaming of frosty dawns,
Of martial drums, of shrill reveilles,
Like a pale hyacinth slowly faded.

Both from their mothers parted: although it seemed
Their flowing curls, resplendent with boyhood's grace,
Awaited yearningly the tender
Touch of a mother's caressing fingers.

Instead they tossed in darkness, uncomforted,
Young but forsaken, and at their obsequies
No sound of their dear native language
Offered them tributes of love and glory.

Not this, O gloomy son of Hortensia,
Not this was thy proud hope for thy little one!
The King of Rome's sad fate be far from
Him, was thy prayer in the ears of Paris.

From Sevastopol white-pinioned Victory
And Peace, her sister, soothed with a whirr of wings
Thy babe to sleep: all Europe wondered:
Flashed like a beacon the stately Column.

And yet December's mud is incarnadined,
Yet are the mists of Brumaire perfidious:
Trees in such atmosphere will wither,
Or is their fruitage but dust and poison.

O solitary house of Ajaccio,
O'er which the tall green oaks spread their foliage!
Behind it rise the hills serenely,
And ever ocean before it thunders.

There lived Letizia, whose fair Italian
Name shall betoken sorrow for centuries
There lived she, bride and happy mother,
Ah, but for too brief a season! Thither,

When thrones lay crushed beneath thy last thunderbolt,
When to the nations just laws were giv'n again,
Thou should'st, great Consul, have withdrawn thee
Home to the sea and the God thou trustedst.

Now like some household ghost Both Letizia
Haunt the forsaken home: no imperial
Splendours engirdled her: thou dweltest,
Corsican mother, 'mid tombs and altars.

Her son the eagle-eyed man of destiny,
Her daughters like Aurora for loveliness,
Her eager, hope-inspired grandsons—
All are dead, all from her breast far sundered.

She stands by night, that Corsican Niobe,
Stands at the threshold whence at their baptism
Her sons went forth from her, and stretcheth
Proudly her arms o'er the wild sea-water,

And calleth, calleth, if from America,
From England, from parched Africa e'en but one
Of all her tragic offspring, tossed by
Death, should find haven in her yearning bosom.

To Giuseppe Garibaldi
(3rd November 1880)

FIRST of the dismal host, unaccompanied,
Rode the Dictator silently, wrapped in thought;
Grey, cheerless, cold, the earth and heaven
Sullenly, gloomily round him lowered.

Clear through the stillness echoed his horse's hoof
Splashing the mud; behind him a measured tramp
Resounds of marching feet, and stifled
Sighs in the night of some breast heroic.

But from the corpse-strewn soil of the battlefield,
But from the sod dyed crimson with blood, where'er
Lay stretched amid that dreadful carnage,
Mothers of Italy, thy beloved ones,

Leapt upward flames like stars to the firmament,
Streamed upward voices chanting victoriously,
Shone forth the vision of Rome triumphant,
Swept down the breezes the thund'rous pan:

"Mentana saw the shame of the centuries
From Peter's fatal union with Csar rise:
Thou halt, Garibaldi, in Mentana
Peter and Cæsar beneath thee trampled.

"Come, O thou splendid rebel of Aspromont,
Mentana's haughty champion, we call to thee;
Tell tales of Rome, tales of Palermo,
Housed on the Capitol, to Camillus."

Thus spirit voices sang from Italian
Skies to his inmost soul solemn prophesies
That day when cowards barked against him,
Curs that a slash of the whip would scatter.

Thou art to-day the idol of Italy,
And Rome renewed hails thee her new Romulus:
Godlike ascendent thou: and never
Shall the long silence of death enfold thee.

Over the common gulf of men's souls art thou,
Towering resplendent, called by the centuries
To take thy seat in that high Council
Formed of our Italy's native Godheads.

Thou dust ascend: and Dante to Virgil cries:
"Hero of nobler mould ne'er imagined we";
And Livy smiling answers: "Poets,
History makes him her own for ever.

"Yea, he belongs to Italy's history,
This hardy scion sprung of Liguria,
In justice rooted deep, who gazeth
Upward to heights of sublime ideals."

Glory to thee, O Father! Thy lion-heart
Breathes in grim Etna's thunderous lava-streams;
It breathes in Alpine storms, for ever
Battling with barbarous kings and tyrants.

Thy childlike heart shines in the cerulean
Smile of the ocean, heav'n, and the blossoming
Spring-seasons that scatter sweet flowers
Over the marble-built tombs of heroes.

THE ROCK AT QUARTO

CLEAVING the quiet water a short rock-rib
Juts forth; behind it copses of laurel-trees,
Thick-foliaged, murmuring softly,
Scatter their scents on the wind of evening.

Before it, full-faced, perfect, most beautiful,
Shineth the moon, and near her the lovely star
Of Venus, with quick throbs of splendour,
Glows from the innermost depths of heaven.

From such a peaceful nook might a man push forth
In some frail bark with one he loved, secretly
Enjoying the bliss of sweet converse,
Lulled by the zephyrs, his mistress by him

Gazing the while intent on the star of Love.
Italia, Italia, mistress of centuries,
Of prophets and martyrs the mistress,
Widow renowned for thy matchless sorrow,

From here pushed forth thy faithful one, seeking thee
Over the ocean. Wrapping the puncio
About his lion-neck, his shoulders
Girt with the sword that at Rome he wielded,

Stood Garibaldi. Shadow-like, silently,
By tens, by fives, mysterious companies
Emerged from the gloom, and then vanished,
Destined to work thy revenge—the Thousand,

Sweeping like pirates swift on their prey: as yet
Unknown to thee, O Italy, sailed they forth,
For thee begging death from the heavens,
Death from the ocean, yea, death from brethren.

Proudly afar shone Genova's citadel,
Rearing her stately marble-built palaces,
Starlike with clustered lights, and distant
Music that died on the moonlit waters.

O House, where Genius, mighty, prophetical,
Bade Pisacane steer on his fateful path
To Naples, O dwelling whence Byron
Thirsted for valiant Missolonghi!

Those marble heights were crowned with Olympian
Glory upon that eve of the fifth of May.
Lo, great as the sacrifice offered,
Great was the victory, O ye Muses.

Pure star of Venus, star of our Italy,
Star of our Cæsar, fair was thy smile that night:
Sure never. a Springtime more holy
Did'st thou illumine for hearts Italian

Since long ago Aeneas' ship silently,
Big with the future, breasted the Tiber stream,
And Pallas was slain near the hills, which
Witnessed the towers of Rome arising.

To the Queen
(20th November 1878)

WHENCE tamest thou? What age left us heir
To thee so gentle and so fair?
     My Queen, what songs of sacred poets
Have I once read and beheld thee there?

In castles, where the Northern race,
Blue-eyed, fair-haired, grew brown of face
     'Neath Latin suns, and knightly minstrels
In new verse strove for their ladies' grace?

When high-born maidens paled with fear
The rhythmic monotone to hear,
     And turned dark, tearful eyes to Heaven,
And prayed, Be not with their sin severe.'

Or saw I thee in those brief days
When Italy was fair with May's
     Own loveliness, when all the nation
Awoke engentled? And in Love's praise

Embattled house and street shone bright
With flowers and marble and sunlight,
     And Dante sang: O cloudlet smiling,
The while Love veileth thee from my sight! '

As in young April's sky doth glow
The star of Venus and below
     Stretch Alpine heights, her mild beams striking
A golden glory across the snow,

Smiling on huts where poor men dwell,
Smiling on fertile vale and fell,
     And in the poplar shade awaking
The nightingales of their love to tell:

So dost thou flash forth, far descried,
Fair, diamond-crowned; and filled with pride
     In thee, the people all acclaim thee
As men rejoice in a maiden bride.

Young girls that gaze at thee with sweet,
Half-tearful smile, as if to greet
    An elder sister, stretch forth shyly
Their arms and cry to thee: Marguerite.'

To thee th' Alcaic verse, free born
'Mid civic strife, and taught to scorn
    All tyrants, flies, and thrice encircles
Thy hair with wings, that no storms have torn,

And sings: Long live thou, O renowned
Fair Lady, whom the Graces crowned,
    In whose soft voice all tones of tender
And loving sympathy sweetly sound.

"Live long as flit o'er Italy
Shapes limned against the evening sky
    By Raphael, long as 'mid the laurels
The sweet canzoni of Petrarch sigh."

At the Station
On an Autumn Morning

OH, how the blinking station lamps drowsily
Stretch in a long line yonder behind the trees!
    Their light, through boughs that drip with raindrops,
    Sleepily gapes on the mud beneath them.

Hard by, the engine peevishly, piercingly,
Stridently hisses; o'er us the leaden sky
    Low lowers, and the autumn morning
    Looms like a limitless dream-world round us.

Whither and wherefore move with such feverish
Haste to the gloomy carriages folk that seem
    So silent and absorbed? What unknown
    Sorrows or hopes unattained torment them?

Thou, too, with thoughtful mien to the guard givest
Thy ticket, Lydia, which he abruptly clips;
    As unto swift-winged Time thou givest
    Youth and its fondly remembered pleasures.

Moving along the line of black coaches go
Black-hooded watchmen, shadow-like, carrying
    In one hand dim lanterns, in the other
    Gripping the hammers of iron wherewith

They test the iron brakes, that return a long,
Dismal metallic clang: from the depth of my
    Sad heart a weary echo answers
    Mournfully, seeming to rack the heart-strings.

And each successive roughly slammed carriage-door
Strikes like an insult: mockery seems the last
    Quick call that rings out down the platform:
    Fiercely the rain on the windows rattles.

And now within the monster his iron soul
Stirs itself: panting, shaking, he openeth
    His flaming eyes: huge through the darkness
    Breathes he the steam, which all heav'n defieth.

On moves th' unholy monster: in cruel flight
Beating his wings he beareth my love away.
Alas, the pale face 'neath the black veil
Smiling farewell in the darkness fadeth.

O exquisite pale face, like a rose in bloom,
O starlike eyes that soothe me with peace,
O white, Pure forehead, shaded by abundant
Tresses, so sweetly towards me bending!

Once at thy smile life thrilled thro' the tepid air,
Thrilled through me summer's magic: I have beheld
The merry sun of June with radiant
Kisses caressing thy tender cheek and

Glinting upon the coils of thy chestnut hair:
Yet round thy gentle form like an aureole
My dreams, more lovely than the sunlight,
Hovered and girt thee about with glory.

Now through the rain and darkness I turn my face
Homeward, and fain would mingle myself with them:
I reel, as drunkards reel, and touch my
Limbs lest I deem myself, too, a phantom.

Oh, how the leaves are falling, are falling, chill,
Silent, relentless, weighing my spirit down!
Methinks that in the world November
Reigneth alone for all men for ever.

Better for whom all feeling of life is dead,
Better these gloomy shades, this obscurity:
I yearn, I yearn to sink unconscious
Lost in a languid eternal slumber.

At the Table of a Friend

SUN-GOD, never from skies, which in earliest
Infancy beam'd on me, shone a radiance
So welcome as thy light to-day poured
O'er the piazzas of old Livorno.

Wine-God, never did thy chalices brim o'er
With genial warmth so generous, benign,
As this cup I drain now to my friend,
Fondly the wild Apennines recalling.

O grant, God of Light, grant, Bromios, that he
And I, unhurt of soul, still accompanied
By Love, with harps still tuned, descend—there
Where Horace is—to reposeful Hades!

But on the children smile ye good auguries,
Who, like blossoms, so sweetly adorn the board;
To their mothers give peace; to bold youths
Glory, love, and happiness without end.

EGLE

GREY in the winter morning, o'ergrown with laurel and ivy,
Sadly the ruined tombs stand by the Appian Way.

High in the clear blue spaces of Heaven, yet dripping with raindrops,
Luminous snow-white clouds blot out the sun and the day.

Egle, upturning her face in the cool, calm air of the morning
Sweet with the promise of spring, gazes intent on the sky—

Gazes; and over those ancient tombs the light of her forehead,
More than the beams of the sun, brightens the clouds that pass by.

A March Song

E'EN as a woman in travail, whom the shades of sleep
Descending slowly, slowly overwhelm at last,
Lies all dishevelled, panting on her bridal bed,
While sighs and broken words chase each other across her lips
And sudden waves of colour flush her pallid face,

So lies the Earth now; for the moving shadows drift
Across the greensward chequered with the pale sunlight,
And the moist breezes sway the peach and almond-trees,
Blossoming in pink and white, until the blossoms fall:
From every pore the brown soil breathes a song to Spring

"Hither, arising from your ocean pastures, come,
Kine of the heavens, ye herds of grey and snow-white clouds!
From swollen breasts rain down your milk on hill and plain,
Smiling beneath you while they clothe themselves in green,
And on the woodland, throbbing with new life again!"

So sing the flowers, awakened from their winter sleep,
So sing the bursting buds from every twig and bough,
And roots, which eagerly strike deeper in the soil:
So from the mould'ring bones of those long dead arise
Germs of new life, singing their resurrection song.

Hark, the stream crashes, the thunder roars among the hills,
The curious heifer peers forth from his dripping stall I
Hark to the cock who crows and proudly flaps his wings;
Deep in the orchard sounds the cuckoo's sighing note,
And baby feet dance joyously upon the lawn.

O stalwart shoulders, bow yourselves to work again!
O hearts of youth and maiden, dream sweet dreams of love!
Wings of the Imagination, fledge yourselves for flight!
Tumultuous desires, now break all barriers down!
Spring comes again, and shall come through the centuries.

THE MOTHER
(A GROUP BY ADRIAN CECIONI)

HER surely Dawn, whose blush biddeth husbandmen
Hasten to fields yet grey in the dusky light,
Beheld with rapid feet unshodden
Pass 'mid the dewy, sweet-scented hayfields.

Bowing her strong back over the yellow-tressed
Furrows, the elm-trees white with the summer dust
Have heard her, carolling at midday,
Challenge the raucous hillside cicalas.

And when from toil she lifted her swelling breast,
Face sun-embrowned, and dark locks, O Tuscany,
Thy vesper lights have touched with flaming
Gold all the lines of her stalwart beauty.

Strong mother now, she dandles her little one,
Strong like herself: full fed from her naked breasts
She dandles him on high, and sweetly
Prattles to him, as he fixes eager.

Eyes on the shining eyes of his mother, while
Each tiny limb is restlessly quivering
And fingers seek her face: the mother
Flings herself laughing, all love, towards him.

Where'er she gazes, home with its happy toil
Greets her: the swaying corn on the green hill-slope,
The lowing cattle, and the crested
Cock in the threshing-floor proudly crowing.

Such are the blessed visions, O Adrian,
Wherewith great Nature comforts the souls of all
Those strong sons of hers who for her sake
Scorn, what the crowd love, mere husks of glory.

Wherefore, stern sculptor, thou hast enshrined in thy
Marble a lofty hope for the centuries.
When shall all men find joy in labour?
When shall they love and be loved securely?

When shall a common folk of free citizens
Cry as they gaze at the Sun: "Oh, shine down upon
Not sloth, neither wars waged by tyrants,
But the mild justice of equal labour"?

ON THE MARRIAGE OF MY DAUGHTER

MY darling, born when o'er the poor
    Home of my youth Hope fluttered by,
    As a bird flies, when proudly I
Knocked at the unknown Future's door,

Now that my foot I firmly place
    Upon the goal I've fought to reach,
    And all around me hoarsely screech
A brood of flattering popinjays,

My dove, a timid yearning fills
    Thy heart o'er Apennine to fleet,
    And build a new nest in the sweet
Air of thy native Tuscan hills.

Thou goest with love, with stainless faith,
    With joy thou goest. Thy veil that flies
    My Muse beholds with tearful eyes,
And sadly dreams, yet nothing saith:

Dreams of those days when thou, a child,
    Did'st pluck flowers 'neath the acacia-tree,
    Thy tiny hand in hers, while she
In heav'n saw shapes and phantoms wild:

Dreams of the days when round thy hair
    Crept those fierce poems that shot red sparks
    Of hatred 'gainst our oligarchs,
Our folk too base to do or dare.

And thou wast growing a thoughtful maid
    When she with courage that knew no fear
    Had stormed the Hills of Art, and there Her
Garibaldian flag displayed.

She looks and ponders. Would she fain
    Retrace with thee the path of years,
    And in thy children's smiles and tears
Dream all the old sweet dreams again?

Or were it better to fight on
    Until the last dread summons calls?
    Then, daughter—for to heaven's halls
No Beatrice hath before me gone—

Then there, where once Greek Homer passed
    And Christian Dante, may thy dear
    Familiar tones, thy soft glance cheer
And comfort me until the last.

BY THE URN OF PERCY BYSSHE SHELLEY

LALAGE, well do I know the dreams that arise in thy bosom,
For a beauty long perished from earth is the quest of thy
    wandering gaze.

Vain are the joys of the present, they come and they fade like a
    blossom;
Only in death dwells the truth and loveliness but in past days.

Lo, on the mount of the centuries Clio hath nimbly descended,
And bursts into song as she spreads her magnificent wings to the sky.

Beneath her the world's vast graveyard extends, all bathed in the
    splendid
Rays of the sun, that illumine her form as she towers on high

In the dawn of an age that is new. O poems that I dreamed in the
    tearless
Years of my youth, fly now to the loves that ye worshipped of old;

Thro' the heaven, thro' the heaven serene fly westward unfettered
    and fearless,
Where the beautiful Island of Dreams glows like a jewel of gold.

There wander the heroes majestic: tall Siegfried and fair-haired
    Achilles,
Yet grasping their spears as they sing by the shores of the echoing
    sea;

Ophelia, escaped from her wan-faced prince, to the one giveth lilies,
The other greets Iphigenia, from the knife and the altar set free;

Under a green-robed oak-tree stout Roland with Hector converses,
The great brand Durendala with gold and with jewels doth blaze;

While Andromache clasps to her bosom again the son that she
    nurses,
Alda the Fair on the fierce Emperor doth motionless gaze;

With the wandering Oedipus white-haired Lear of past sorrow is
     speaking,
And dim-eyed Oedipus still from his search for the Sphinx cannot
     cease;

Cordelia the dutiful cries: Fair Antigone, thee was I seeking.
     Grecian sister, O come I Let us sing to our fathers of peace ';

Helen, with Iseult beside her, 'neath the myrtles thoughtfully paces,
Their tresses of gold catch the gleam of the skies where the sunset is
     red;

Helen looks out to the sea: King Mark sweet Iseult embraces,
And bowed on his flowing beard reposes her golden head.

There with the Scottish Queen on the moonlit, magical beaches
Stands Clytemnestra: their round white arms to the sea-waves are
     bent;

But the sea flows backward in wrath from each bloodstained hand
     ere it reaches
The cleansing tide, and the cliffs but re-echo their bitter lament.

O fortunate island, far distant, unknown of poor labouring mortals,
Island of beautiful women, isle of heroical men,

Island of poets! The ocean uptosses its foam at they portals,
And thy sunset skies are the haven of birds that are strange to our ken.

There the roll of the Epic swells with a deep-toned musical thunder,
Shaking the laurels as when o'er the plain the May hurricanes pass,

Or when Wagner the mighty moves all hearts to tremble and
     wonder,
Breathing a thousand souls into the ringing brass.

Ah, but no modern poet e'er reached those ineffable places,
Only perchance thou, Shelley, whom a spirit Titanic inspires,

Who art fair with a virginal beauty: from Thetis' yearning embraces
Sophocles snatched thee, and placed thee amid those heroical choirs.

O heart of hearts, o'er this urn, thy cold, uncongenial prison,
The warm spring blossoms again with the fragrance of flower and
    fruit.

O heart of hearts, thy divine great father, the Sun, hath arisen,
And lovingly bathes thee in light, poor heart that for ever art mute.

Freshly murmur the pines to the breezes that sweep o'er the city
Poet of liberty, answer, where art thou? Dost hear when we call?

Where art thou? Dost hearken? Mine eyes are wet with the tears of
    my pity
As I gaze o'er the mournful Campagna beyond the Aurelian wall.

A Snow-Storm

LARGE, slow snowflakes fall from an ashen heaven: the noisy
Hum and hubbub of life no more go up from the town.

Hushed is the cry of the vendor of herbs, the rumble of waggons,
Hushed are the voices that sang blithely of youth and of love.

Harsh thro' the throbbing air the chimes from the tower o'er the market
Moan, like the sigh of a world far from the daylight withdrawn.

Tap on the frosted panes, birdlike, forlorn, the beloved
Ghosts of old friends who return, calling on me to depart.

Soon, dear ones, very soon—O strong heart, calm thyself—I too
Shall to the silence descend, lay me to rest in the gloom.

CONGEDO

LET kings present as sign of grace
A golden necklace to the bard:
Let jesters, when the populace
Clap hands and shout, have their reward.

Prize for my verse, which eagerly
Betwixt the Past and Future flies,
One brimming cup to Friendship I
Demand, one smile from Beauty's eyes.

Like memory of an April morn
How pure is Beauty's smile; how sweet
To one whom winged age cloth warn
That his ninth lustre's near complete.

And 'mid the cups by Friendship crowned
Serene, O Plato, as beneath
Ilissus' plane-trees he was found
By thee, doth flit the form of Death.

A TRANSLATION

A Summer Night
(From Klopstock)

IN the night-time, when the splendour of the moon
Sheds a glory o'er the woods and the perfumes
Of the linden-trees are wafted
On the cool, fragrant air,

Then do thoughts of those I loved who now are dead
Overshadow me awhile, and the twilight
Ever deepens, and I cannot
Smell the scent of the leaves.

Long ago, ye Dead, I shared it all with you,
All the perfumes and the coolness of twilight,
And fair nature seemed e'en fairer
'Neath the beams of the moon.

from
RIME E RITMI

To the Signorina Maria A.

TELL me, little maiden,
    Can verse mean aught to thee?

Only from hearts o'erladen,
    O happy little maiden,
    Where pain all joy doth deaden,
    Escapeth poetry.

How then, dear little maiden,
    Can verse mean aught to thee?

Jaufré Rudel

FROM Lebanon red morning glances
On billows that foam and toss sunwards;
From Cyprus with white sails advances
The Crusader ship ever onwards.
    Rudél, the young prince of Blaye, lies on
The deck, and with fever doth wrestle;
His swimming eyes scan the horizon
For the turrets of Tripoli's castle.

When the far Asian coastline is sighted
His familiar canzone he singeth:
"O fair foreign Love, to whom plighted
My troth is, I'm heart-sick for thee."
    Its flight a grey halcyon wingeth,
And prolongs the sweet note of repining;
The sun, on the white canvas shining,
In mist veils his face from the sea.

The vessel with furled sails lies gladly
At rest in the port. Then descendeth
Young Bertrand: alone and full sadly
His way up the hillside he wendeth.
    Round Rudél's escutcheon a slender
Funereal scarf doth he wind;
To the castle then hastes: "Melisenda
Of Tripoli where shall I find?

"I come as love's messenger hither,
I come as death's messenger: duty
And love bid me enter here, whither
I am sent by Rudél, lord of Blaye.
    Men spake unto him of thy beauty;
Unseen he did love thee, did sing thee:
He comes, he is dying. I bring thee
Thy true poet's greeting to-day."

The lady gazed long on the squire,
Deep plunged in her thoughts, then, deciding,
She rose, with a black veil the fire
Of her eyes and her loveliness hiding.
    "Sir squire," said she quickly, "come, show me
Where Jaufré lies dying. Thou waitest
Not vainly, true bard thou shalt know me,
Shalt hear love's first words and love's latest."

'Neath a stately pavilion extended
Lay Jaufré in sight of the ocean,
And, with notes of his canzone blended,
Breathed forth the last wish of his heart.
    "O God, who did'st for my devotion
Create this far Love, be it given
Unto me, clasped at last in the heaven
Of her arms, from this life to depart."

Meanwhile with young Bertrand drew nigher
She on whom all this prayer was centred,
And, hearing his last notes expire,
Wept in pity awhile ere she entered.
    Then straightway the veil that did cover
Her face she tore off, and drew near
With quick steps to the couch of her lover.
"Look, Jaufré," she said, "I am here."

In a moment the prince turned, upraising
His breast on the rugs strewn to soften
The couch: at those fair features gazing
Entranced, he breathed one long sigh.
    "Are these the bright eyes that so often
Love promised should shine on me waking?
Is this the fair brow to which, breaking
All barriers, my fond dreams would fly?"

As when on a May night beclouded
The moon her white radiance is streaming
O'er the world that in slumber lies shrouded,
And the air with night perfumes is teeming,
    E'en so with a wondrous completeness
His pain by her beauty was ended,
And comfort divine in its sweetness
On the dying man's spirit descended.

"Ah, lady, what's life and its glory?
A dream and a shadow soon over.
Life reaches its end like a story;
'Tis love that alone lasts for aye.
    Embrace then thy sorrowful lover!
At the Last Day these arms shall receive thee.
And now, Melisenda, I give thee
My soul in one kiss ere I die."

The countess stooped low as she pressed him
To her bosom in speechless emotion,
Then thrice with the kiss of love kissed him
With pale lips that trembled to his.
    As it dipped to the glittering ocean
The sun from a heaven unclouded
Lit her tresses of gold that enshrouded
The bard, who had died in the kiss.

PIEDMONT

AMONG the jagged, glittering peaks
The chamois bounds: woods bend and crack,
Swept by the ice-born avalanche
    Adown its thundering track.

But from the silent azure sails
The eagle slowly into sight,
And through the sunshine wheeling spreads
    His dark and solemn flight.

Hail, Piedmont! With a music sad
Yet echoing thund'rous as thine own
Brave people's epic battle-songs,
    The mountain-streams leap down.

Leap downward swift and bold as thine
Own hundred regiments, to seek
Out towns and villages with whom
    Of thy renown to speak:

Ancient Aosta, cloaked in royal
Ramparts, barring the foeman's march,
Who o'er barbarian mansions still
    Lifts her imperial arch;

Ivrea the fair, whose rose-red towers
Dream, mirrored in blue Dora's breast,
While o'er her Blooms King Arduin's ghost,
    The ghost that will not rest;

Biella, who 'twixt green plain and hill
Naught but the fertile valley sees,
Rejoicing in her arms and ploughs
    And smoking furnaces:

Strong, patient Cuneo, Mondovi
That on soft meadow-slopes reclines,
And Aleramo boasting of
    His castle and his vines;

And by Superga victory-crowned
Turin the royal, amid her great,
Glad choir of Alpine giants, and then
    Asti's republic state.

Proud of her slaughtered Goths and proud
If Frederick's wrath, she, Piedmont, gave
To thee Alfieri's stern new song,
    Born of her crashing wave.

That great one came like the great bird
Whence he was named: untiringly,
Fiercely o'er the low land he flew,
    "Italy, Italy"

Crying to spirits downtrodden, to ears
Unused to hear, to hearts grown slack;
And "Italy" Ravenna's tomb
    And Arquà's answered back.

Beneath his flight through all the dark
Peninsula's graveyard the dry
Bones rattled, yearning for their swords
    Once more to fight, to die.

"Italy, Italy": the dead
Folk rose again with battle-shout;
And, lo, a king drew sword, whose heart
    And pale face marked him out

Death's victim. Oh, portentous year,
Oh, springtime of this land of ours,
Oh, days—oh, latest days of May
    Fair with a thousand flowers,

Oh, sound of the first Italian triumph,
That pierced my boyish heart!
Whence I, Italy's seer in fairer times,
    Grey-haired to-day, now try

To sing thee, king of my fresh youth,
King for so long bewailed, unblest,
Who rode forth, sword in hand, sackcloth
   Upon thy Christian breast,

Italian Hamlet. 'Neath the fire
And steel of Piedmont, 'neath the blow
Aosta struck, 'neath Cuneo's nerve,
   Melted the vanquished foe.

Faintly behind the Austrian rout
The last gun's thunder died away:
The King rode down towards the West,
   Where sank the star of day;

And to the horsemen, smoke-begrimed,
Victorious, who towards him sped,
From an unfolded note the words
   "Peschiera's ours," he read.

From breasts that swelled with pride of race,
Savoy's fair standards waving high,
How deafening rose one shout: "Long live
   The King of Italy!"

The Lombard plain flamed with bright gold,
By the red sunset glorified:
The lake of Virgil quivered, like
   The veil of a young bride

Oped to the kiss of promised love.
Eyes fixed, pale-faced, on horseback stayed
The King unmoved: alone he saw
   The Trocadero's shade.

For him Novara's fogs, for him
Oporto waited, bourne of all
His failures. Oh, lone House beside
   The Douro, 'mid thy tall

Chestnuts, who hear'st the Atlantic surge
Before thee, while camellias grow
By thy fresh streams, how coldly thou
    Did'st harbour such deep woe!

He lay a-dying: in that twilight
Between two lives, when sense doth cease,
The King beheld a wondrous vision:
    The Mariner of Nice,

Fair-haired, spurred from Janiculum
'Gainst Gaulish outrage: like a red,
Sun-smitten carbuncle round him flamed
    Blood by Italians shed.

In the dim eyes gathered a tear,
Flickered a faint smile. Then a band
Of spirits flew down from Heaven, and round
    The dead King took their stand.

Santorre of Santarosa, who
In Alexandria first outspread
The Tricolour, in Pylos now
    Sleeping, O Piedmont, led

Those spirits, who all bore up to God
Charles Albert's soul. "Behold him, Lord,
The King our foe, the King our scourge,
    The man whom we abhorred:

"He, too, hath died now, as we died,
For Italy. To us restore
Our land! To quick and dead, by all
    The plains that reek with gore,

"By all the sorrow which on hut
And palace both alike hath come,
Oh, God, by our past deeds of fame,
    Our present martyrdom,

"Restore to that brave, pleading dust,
To this exultant angel band,
Their country; to the Italian folk
    Th' Italian Fatherland."

CADORE

I

GREAT art thou. Sunlike, shining eternally,
Thy rainbow colours comfort the world of men.
Idealised, youthful for ever,
Nature doth smile in the forms thy genius

Pictured. The rose-red glow of thy phantasies
Flashed o'er that grim, tumultuous century,
And hushed was the clash of those warring
Nations; they paused to look upward, wond'ring.

And he, the Flemish Cæsar, the passionless
Destroyer, who sacked Rome and our Italy,
Forgetting his majesty, stooped to
Pick up for thee from the floor thy pencils.

Say, dost thou sleep, O ancient one, 'neath the weight
Of Austrian marbles where the grey Fran looms
Around thee, or dost thou now wander,
Spirit diffused, o'er thy native mountains,

Here, where on thee, whose forehead Olympian
One hundred years of calm life engarlanded,
'Mid white clouds doth smile the cerulean
Sky, and doth woo thee with fragrant kisses?

Yea, thou art great. And yet yonder humble stone
With more compelling magic doth call to me;
The bold face of yon youth defiant
Claims from me songs in the classic measure.

Tell me, O godlike youth, whom defiest thou?
Battle and fate and terrible onset of
A thousand 'gainst one thou defiest,
Spirit heroical, Pietro Calvi.

Yea, e'en so long as Piave through wild ravines
In the eternal flight of the centuries
Flows downward and buffets the Adrian
Sea with the wrack of her dark-stemmed forests,

Which to Saint Mark of old gave his turreted
War-galleys yonder 'mid the Echinades;
So long as the westering sun doth
Tinge the pale Dolomite's distant spires,

Making the mountains, loved by Vecellio,
His Marmarole glisten at eventide
Rose-red, a dream-palace, where spirit
Forms and veiled Destinies float in splendour:

So long, O Calvi, so long may thy dread name
Live unforgotten, peal like a trumpet-call
To brave hearts, and pulse in the pallid
Cheeks of our youths as they arm to battle.

II

Not with the oat of Arcadian swains do I sing thee, Cadore,
        Blending with murmur of wind and rill;
Thee do I hymn in heroic verse, that blends with the thunder
        Of guns heard in the vales below.

Oh, that second of May, when he leapt on the parapet bounding
        The road by Austria's frontier!
Captain Pietro Calvi—the bullets whistled around him—
        Fair-haired, erect, immovable,

Lifts on the point of his sword, while he glares at the foe in defiance,
        The note surrend'ring Udine:
High in his left hand waves he a red scarf, signal of battle,
        Of war and battle to the death.

Pelmo and Antelao, beholding that deed of a hero,
        Shake free from clouds their hoary crests,
Like unto giants primeval, who, tossing the plumes of their helmets,
        Stand by and gaze upon the fight.

Like unto shields of heroes, which flash in the sagas of minstrels
        Along the astonied centuries,
Glistening white and pure in the rays of the sun as he climbeth
        The sky their sparkling glaciers shine.

Sun of the glories of olden days, with how burning an ardour
	Dost thou embrace Alps, streams, and men!
Thou thro' the sod beneath the gloomy forests of pine-trees
	Dost penetrate and wake the dead.

"Sons, o'er our mouldering bones smite down, smite down the invader,
	Barbarian, our eternal foe!
Crags, crash down from the snows stained red with our blood!
		Avalanches,
		Annihilate him utterly!"

So from mountain to mountain re-echoes the voice of the heroes
	Who at Rusecco fought and died,
And from town unto town it swells ever louder; like thunder
	The breezes catch and pass it on.

Blithely they rush to arms the youths of Titian's village
	With battle-shout of "Italy";
Smiling the women lean o'er the black wooden balconies gay with
	Carnations and geraniums.

Mirthful Pieve, that nestles 'mid smiling hills and hearkens
	To Piave thund'ring far below
Lovely Auronzo, stretched far out o'er the plain 'mid her waters
	'Neath gloomy Mount Ajarnola,

And sunny Lorenzago, 'mid sloping meadows, the mistress
	Of the wide dale on either hand,
All the green Comelico dotted with hamlets half hidden
	Among the fir-trees and the pines,

And other towns, and yet others, from smiling woodland and pasture
	Send forth their fathers and their sons;
Guns are seized, and spears and pruning-hooks brandished: the echoes
	Are wakened by the shepherd's horn.

Plucked from the Altar, the ancient banner is borne which at Valle
	Beheld another Austrian rout,
Bidding the heroes hail: at a new sun, at a new peril
	The old Venetian lion roars.

Hark! a faint, far sound on the breeze, ever nearer, distincter
It swells, clangs, clashes tumultuous;
Sound of weeping and calling, of shrieking, of praying, of goading
To frenzy, insistent, terrible.

"What does it mean?" demandeth the foe, who seeketh a parley,
With questioning and startled gaze.
"They are the bells of the people of Italy," calm came the answer;
"For our death or for yours they ring."

Ah, Pietro Calvi, on the plain by Mantua's trenches
When seven years have passed shall Death
Seize thee—thee, who camest in quest of her, e'en as an exile
Steals back in secret to his bride.

As on the Austrian guns, so now on the Austrian gibbet
He gazeth, glad, unflinching, calm,
Grateful unto the foe who condemn him to pass as a soldier
To join the Holy Host of Dead.

Never a nobler soul hast thou launched at Italy's future,
Released from vile imprisonment,
Belfiore, black pit, 'neath th' Austrian gallows: Belfiore,
Bright altar of the martyrs now.

Oh, if ever a man, calling Italy mother, forget thee,
May his adulterous bed bring forth
Such as shall trample him down in the mire; from the gods of his
household
Thrust out in old age, vile, abhorred!

And in the heart, in the brain, in the blood of him who denieth
His country, may some ghastly power
Urge him to suicide! and from his mouth, blaspheming, repulsive,
May a green toad exude its slime.

III
To thee returneth, e'en as the Bird of Jove
When with a struggling snake he hath gorged himself
Sails home on wide, motionless pinions,
Home to the sun and his wind-swept eyrie,

To thee this sacred song of the fatherland
Turns home, Cadore. Swelling melodiously,
The gradual murmur of pine-trees
'Neath the pale beams of the white Moon-Maiden

Breathes o'er the magic sleep of thy waters with
Long-drawn caresses. Thy happy villages
Now blossom with flaxen-haired children:
On the o'erhanging cliff-edges stalwart

Girls cut the hay 'mid laughter and song, their bright
Tresses confined in black scarves, and rapidly
Their blue eyes with keen glances sparkle:
And by precipitous mountain pathways

The carter drives his team of three horses down,
Dragging a load of pine-trunks, and all the air
Is filled with their fragrance, and round the
Weir swarm the woodmen of Perarolo.

Hark, through the mists enwreathing the mountain-tops
Thunders the chase; and, sure hit, the chamois falls—
Ay, falls as the foe, when our country
Calls on her sons to defend her, falleth.

Pietro Calvi's spirit I seek to snatch
From thee, Cadore, and on the wings of song
Throughout the peninsula send it
Herald-like:—"Ah, to ill purpose wakened,

"Deem'st thou the Alps a pillow encouraging
Slumber and dreams of treach'rous adultery?
Up, sluggard, and finish thy warfare!
Up, for the cock of the War-God croweth!'

Not until Marius climb o'er the Alps again,
And on the twin seas gazette Duilius,
Shalt thou be appeased, O Cadore,
Shall we demand from thee Titian's spirit.

Then on the shining, spoil-enriched
Capitol Splendid with new laws; ay, on the Capitol
Then let him paint Italy's triumph,
Her new Assumption among the nations.

Funeral of the Guide E. R.

SHATTERED the hand that boldly, without fear,
On glaciers swung the ice-axe! He lies low,
Who tamed the high hills, on yon humble bier.

The train of mourners passes down with slow,
Sad chants from Saxa; while the priests recite:
"Lord, grant him Thine eternal peace to know."

"And may he dwell in everlasting light,"
The women make response: upon the breeze
Death's banner floats among the pines. Now quite

Distinct, now faintlier borne, their dirges seize
The listener's ear: now see we not, now see
The choir winding slowly through the trees.

Forth come they now unto the cemet'ry,
And set the bier down 'mid the crosses ere
The priest cries: "May the Lord have mercy on thee,

"Emil, thou king of all the mountains! Fair
And pure thy spirit was, and every day
To Mary's bosom duly rose thy prayer."

Mindful of fallen sons and those who may
Yet fall, the women, 'neath their black veils bowed
To earth, bewail brave lives thus cast away.

Lo, suddenly the mists, whose sombre shroud
Veiled great Mont Blanc, melt from his ample breast
And in the clear sky form deep banks of cloud,

Through a wide rent of which stands forth confessed
In cruel majesty, precipitous,
Cleaving the azure air with threat'ning crest,

The *Giant's Tooth*, sun-smitten, glorious.

THE CHURCH OF POLENTA

SWAYING and solitary, above
  The hills yon cypress beckons: chance
  Francesca here her burning glance
Once softened to a smile of love.

Sheer stands the cliff, yet threatens not:
  The boatman, glancing up on high,
  Ponders; his oars seem wings that fly
From darkling Adria: yonder cot

Smokes, where the peasant for his rude
  Repast stirs grain like yellow gold
  In the bright cauldron—there, where old
Guido's grim eagle used to brood.

Beauty's the shadow of a flower
  O'er which the white moth Poetry
  Flutters: as in the valley die
A trumpet's echoes, dieth Power.

Time's flight and barbarous ages naught
  Hath conquered, save one thing alone,
  That beacons out the past upon
The coming years—poetic Thought.

There stands the church built when, by name
  Unknown, beneath Rome's yoke still bowed
  Polenta's future lords, endowed
By Dante with eternal fame.

Knelt Dante here in ages gone?
  With lofty brow, which once had seen
  God's face, now hidden both hands between,
He wept for his own fair St. John;

And sunlight flashed out o'er the main
  From the vast woods. About him rise
  Bright Forms, his guests from Paradise,
And beat upon the exile's brain.

From these low arches angels sang,
   And through yon white aisle opening to
   The East the psalm *In exitu*
Israel de Ægypto rang.

O many-lived Italian race,
   Where'er day conquers night, where'er
   Flash gleams of your old glory, there
The Poet's influence may ye trace.

But stretched by open tombs through all
   These churches did old men, in frocks
   Of grey, with black, dishevelled locks
Defiled by filthy ashes, call

Upon the ghastly, white-eyed, lean
   Byzantine crucifix, and pray
   For mercy in her evil day
On Rome, the world's deposèd Queen.

From sculptured capitals peered forth,
   Carved by some hand that dimly apes
   The Grecian chisel, horrid Shapes,
Foul Nightmares of the grisly North,

Monstrosities degenerate,
   Born of the lawless East, half seen
   Through flickering lamplight, in obscene
Embraces twisted, glared and spat

Upon the prostrate throng: behind
   The baptist'ry, beyond the font
   A small red devil with horned front
Maliciously gazed down and grinned.

The winter of barbarians roared
   Without o'er hill and plain; the black
   Ships, shooting down their wind-swept track,
Each with a howling god aboard,

Fierce Odin's fire and fury rain
   On towns that smile betwixt two bright
   And glassy seas, and stretch their white
Arms to the Earth-shaker in vain.

Woe upon woe! For onward sweeps
   The Hunnish army, a whirlwind
   Of shaggy-coated steeds; behind,
The gleaner, Death, laughs as he reaps.

Ah, Jesu! Sepulchres unclosed
   Black mouths, and with indignant groans
   Lay e'en the blessèd martyrs' bones
To wind and rain and sun exposed.

Down from each still unstormed redoubt
   The bearded Lombard comes again,
   And with his lance what doth remain—
Ruins, ashes, desert—portions out.

O slaves, despoiled and smitten, yet
   One thing—your Church—is left you!
   This Your home, your tomb, your country is:
Here see ye naught, here all forget.

One day shall those who spoil and smite,
   Themselves, despoiled and smitt'n, come here.
   As at the vintage disappear
Within the seething vats our white

And purple grapes, torn from the vine,
   Which, trampled on and crushed, at length
   By mingling their peculiar strength
Mature into the perfect wine;

So here, before that God who said:
   "Vengeance is Mine, forgive thy foes!"
   The victors and the vanquished—those,
By Queen Theodolinda led

Through prayer to Christ; these, made immune
  From bonds, O Rome, by Gregory
  Thund'ring thy word—united by
Old strength, new love, formed the Commune.

Hail, thou, enterraced high between
  Bertinoro and that sweet plain,
  O'er which, far as the sea, doth reign
Cesena, of brave men the queen!

Hail, little church of this my song!
  O many-lived Italian race,
  Reborn once more, to this dear place,
That mothered thee of old, now throng

To pray: and let the bell ring clear
  Its warning note: from hill to hill
  Let the bell-tower, re-risen, still
Peal o'er the land "Ave Maria."

Ave Maria! When down the air
  That lowly greeting runs, with brow
  Uncovered tiny mortals bow,
Dante and Byron breathe a prayer.

Unseen a slow, sweet melody
  Of flutes thro' earth and heaven flows:
  Is it perchance the souls of those
That have been, are, and yet shall be?

Then doth a slow forgetfulness
  Of weary life, a dreamy sense
  Of deep peace after pain, which vents
Itself in tears, men's souls possess

All things are silent, far and near
  The after-glow fades from the sky;
  Only the swaying tree-tops sigh:
Ave Maria, Ave Maria!

SAINT ABBONDIO

BRILLIANT the sky, as 'twere of diamond made,
Wherethrough unearthly radiance seems to glow;
Like souls love-stricken, in the far distance fade
The mountains, line on line of sparkling snow.

Pale blue amid the tree-tops, gently swayed
By a light breeze, the smoke-wreaths upward go
From cottage roofs: in many a bright cascade
Through emerald grass flows the Madesimo.

Red-gowned the Alpine women pass to keep
Thy feast day, Saint Abbondio; their song,
The stream's, the pine-trees' murmur blend in one.

What smileth there down in the valley deep?
Peace, peace, my heart! Fair is the world, and long
The sleep thou sleepest when brief life is done.

To the Valkyries
For the Funeral of the
Empress-Queen Elizabeth

GOLDEN-HAIRED Valkyries, ye who delight to spur on your horses
    Swimming above the clouds, tresses astream in the wind,

From the monotonous moaning, the dreary drone of the clergy,
    Now, as ye fly past, snatch Wittelsbach's Lady away!

Ah, how terribly Fate thy tottering House o'erwhelmeth!
    How are thy grey hairs, Hapsburg, brought down in woe to
      the grave!

Peace, O ye in the gloom of Arad and Mantua keeping
    Vigil, ye ghostlike shapes, women dishevelled and wild!

Golden-haired even as ye are, O Valkyries, rider of horses
    Even as ye, bear her unto a balmier clime!

Where 'neath lovely Corcyra the azure Ionian crooneth
    Unto the orange groves, dreamily lapping the shore.

Calm o'er the hills of Epirus the white moon riseth, and far as
    Leucas lengthens her torch, tremulous over the waves.

There doth Achilles await her. O Valkyries, purge from her noble
    Bosom the stain of the wound dealt by that villainous blade.

And from her soul, ye gracious, ye healing divinities, purge the
    Scars of her sorrow, the black nightmare of Empire away I

Then let the stainless rose of Bavaria wake to the music,
    Piercing and sweet, of the lyres, unto new harmonies tuned.

Never hath Heine's muse sung sweetlier: whose is the sighing
    Voice that re-echoes his notes from the Leucadian steep?

Peace, unbroken, profound as the calm of Elysian meadows,
    Reigns o'er that ghost-haunted shore, silent, sleep-charmed
      by the moon.

Near a Monastery

FROM yon green, which 'mid th' acacia's brown and crimson leaves
     endeavours
Yet to linger, though no wind hath stirred, itself a leaflet severs:
And it seems a soul is dying,
Shuddering imperceptibly.

Seems the mist a veil of silver o'er the streamlet softly purling;
Through the mist the leaf falls, lost amid the water's rapid whirling.
Ah, what means the feverish sighing
Of the graveyard cypresses?

Suddenly breaks forth the sun, and o'er the morning damps
     prevaileth
And thro' snowy clouds across the azure sky serenely saileth:
See the frowning woods replying,
"'Tis the spring he heraldeth!"

Smile upon me ere the winter wraps my soul in melancholy
Darkness; smile on me, O Poetry divine, O Radiance holy!
Father Homer, hear me crying
Ere the shade o'erwhelmeth me!

CONGEDO

TRICOLOUR blossom,
The stars set in the sea, the sacred fire
Of Poetry is quenched within my bosom.

PART I
of the
CANZONE DI LEGNANO
(1879)

THE PARLIAMENT

I

THE Emperor Frederick was encamped at Como,
And, lo, a messenger, with reins abandoned,
Rode into Milan by the Porta Nuova.
"People of Milan," so he called in passing,
"Bring me with speed to the Consul Gherardo."
They brought him to the Consul in the market;
The messenger bent from his saddle, whispered
A few brief words, and swiftly galloped onward.
Then the Consul Gherardo gave a signal,
"To Parliament" the trumpets shrilly sounded.

II

To Parliament the trumpets shrilly sounded;
For not yet had the stately palace risen
On massive pillars, nor was there a tribune,
Nor tower, nor on the summit of the tower
The bell. Amid the blackened ruins, covered
With flowering thorn-trees, there amid the lowly
Wooden houses in the narrow market,
Beneath the May sun, held the men of Milan
Their Parliament. From doorways and from windows
Stood watching them the women and the children.

III

"Ye gentlemen of Milan," saith the Consul,
"The springtime with its flowers brings the Germans
As oft before. In their own dens the gluttons
Keep Easter, then descend upon the valley.
Through the Engadine two excommunicated
Archbishops have led down the hostile forces.
The fair-haired Empress brought unto her husband
A loyal heart and therewith a fresh army.
Como hath left the league and joined the stronger."
"Let Como be destroyed," the people shouted.

IV

"Ye gentlemen of Milan," saith the Consul,
"The Emperor, having formed his host in Milan,
Leads on his troops to join those that the Marquis
Of Montferrato and Pavia send him.
What will ye do, ye men of Milan? Will ye
From the new dyke wait idly in your armour,
Or send envoys to Cæsar, or in battle
With lance and sword defy the Barbarossa?"
"With lance and sword!" the whole assembly thundered;
"With lance and sword, the Barbarossa, in battle!"

V

And now stepped forward Albert of Giussano:
By a full shoulder's height he towered over
The folk that stood assembled round the consul.
In his vast strength his figure like a tower
Uprose amid the Parliament. His helmet
Hung in his hand, his chestnut hair was floating
About his mighty neck and ample shoulders.
The sun shone full upon his comely features
And glinted in his hair and eyes reflected.
His voice was as the thunder in the Maytime.

VI

"Burghers of Milan, brothers, ye my people,
Remember ye," saith Albert of Giussano,
"The first of March, that day whereon to Lodi
Rode our wan Consuls, and to him, with naked
Swords in their hands, swore fealty and obedience?
Upon the fourth of March we rode three hundred,
And humbly kissed his feet, and laid before him
Our beautiful, our six-and-thirty standards.
Master Guitelmo offered him the keys of
Famished Milan. And it naught availed us."

VII

"Remember ye," saith Albert of Giussano,
"The sixth of March? He would have all before him,
All at his feet—the soldiers, people, standards.
So forth from the three gates the burghers issued:
Came the Carroccio decked for war; thereafter
Great multitudes of people, each man holding
A cross within his hand. From the Carroccio
The trumpets blared for the last time before him;
Towards him from the mast of the Carroccio
The city's standard drooped: he touched its fringes."

VIII

"Remember ye," saith Albert of Giussano,
"How, clothed in weeds of penitence and sackcloth,
Cords knotted round our necks, our feet unshodden,
Our hair with ashes sprinkled, in the mire
We knelt and grovelled, and, our arms outstretching,
Besought him to have mercy? All around him—
Yea, every knight and gentleman around him—
Wept at the sight. He stood, erect and silent,
Beside the imperial shield, and gazed upon us
With hard dry, eyes that glittered like a diamond."

IX

"Remember ye," saith Albert of Giussano,
"Unto our shame returning on the morrow,
How from the street we spied the Empress gazing
Upon us from a lattice? T'wards the lattice
We lifted up our crosses, crying to her:
'O Empress, fair-haired, beautiful, O faithful,
O merciful, have mercy on our women!'
She drew back from the casement. But he bade us
Raze wall and gates of both engirdling ramparts
That so his host might pass arrayed for battle."

X

"Remember ye," saith Albert of Giussano,
"Nine days we waited, and they all departed,
The lord archbishop, all the counts and vassals?
Upon the tenth day came the Ban: " Forth with ye,
O wretches, forth, with women, sons, belongings!
The Emperor doth but eight days' grace allow ye."
And we ran shrieking unto St. Ambrogio,
Embracing there the sepulchres and altars.
Out from the church with women and with children,
Out from the church like scurvy dogs, they chased us."

XI

"Remember ye," saith Albert of Giussano,
"That sad Palm-Sunday? Alas, for Jesus' Passion,
It was the Passion of our Milan also.
For from the Church of the four Saints we witnessed
The thrice a hundred towers of our encircling
Walls crash down one by one; last, through the ruins,
Amid thick clouds of dust, appeared our houses,
Shattered and shivered and annihilated:
They looked like rows of skeletons in a graveyard.
Beneath, the bones were burning of our dead ones."

XII

Thus having spoken, Albert of Giussano
Stood silent, and his eyes with both hands hiding
He wept; yes, in the midst of the assembly
He wept and sobbed, as a child weeps. Then slowly
Throughout the whole assembly passed a murmur,
That swelled into a storm like wild beasts roaring.
The women from the doorways and the windows,
Pale and dishevelled, with their arms extended
And staring eyes, shrieked out to the assembly:
"Death unto him, death to the Barbarossa!"

XIII

"And now behold!" saith Albert of Giussano,
"Behold, I weep no more. Our day is coming,
O men of Milan. Victory must attend us.
Behold, I dry my eyes, and at thee gazing,
Fair Sun of God, I make my vow. To-morrow
By eventide our dead in Purgatory
Shall have sweet news of us. Behold, I swear it,
Be I myself the messenger." But the people
Cried: "Better imperial messengers." And smiling
The sun went down behind the Resegone.

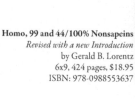

Made in United States
North Haven, CT
11 April 2024

51195568R00136